Music of the Yorkshire Dales

The Pateley Bridge cuckoo had a plaintive note.

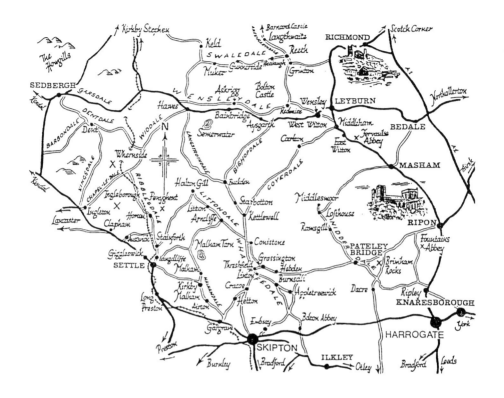

A **Castleberg** Book.

First published in the United Kingdom in 1997.

Copyright © W R Mitchell 1997.

The moral right of the author has been asserted.

ISBN 1 871064 73 2

Typeset in Palacio, printed and bound in the United Kingdom by
Lamberts Printers, Station Road, Settle, North Yorkshire, BD24 9AA.

Published by Castleberg, 18 Yealand Avenue, Giggleswick, Settle,
North Yorkshire, BD24 0AY.

Contents

canvasses of Beethoven's *Pastoral Symphony,* Haydn's *The Seasons*, Delius's *North Country Sketches*, Copland's *Appalachian Spring* or the forbidding wintry landscape of Sibelius's *Tapiola.*

Music in the Yorkshire Dales, a new look at the subject, takes into account what has been added in more recent times, such as, for example, the impact made by the Settle-Carlisle railway. The book is heartily to be recommended.

Dales Methodism was noted for its lively hymn-singing.

Introduction

EDWARD ELGAR, a visitor to Yorkshire Dales in the 1880s, was a composer who in his youth had listened to natural sounds and attempted to reproduce them musically. He is said to have plucked musical themes from the air itself.

In the Dales, as he sauntered forth with his friend Dr Buck of Giggleswick, Elgar would doubtless hear a 'wuthering' wind, the hiss of water pouring over a lip of limestone to fall on well-polished stones. Elgar would hear the baritone voice of the carrion crow but, as an autumnal visitor, he would not have the joy of listening to the pulsating, bubbling trill of a curlew gliding across rough pastureland at the skirts of Ingleborough or Penyghent.

Elgar's experiences of Dales life and scenery were mainly confined to the southern part of what is now the Yorkshire Dales National Park. Writing to Buck in 1888, he proclaimed: "I shall be glad to get a whiff of pure mountain air again."

He loved Pennine waterfalls—but did not see the Tees tripping down its stone staircase at Cauldron Snout or throwing itself from a ledge of whin sill at High Force. Nor, it would seem, did Elgar ever stand beside Aysgarth Falls, in Wensleydale, where the river flows over horizontal limestone steps and has an impressively neat appearance.

Elgar did visit Scaleber, a waterfall tucked away, though close to the road between Settle and Kirkby Malham. His friend Dr Buck would not have the time to show his friend the Strid, in Wharfedale, where a mighty river is confined between banks of dark rock. Elgar was fond of visiting Harrogate, enjoying a morning walk in the flower-decked Valley Gardens. He was taken to the old Cistercian abbey of Fountains, which is dignified even in a ruined state, rising like a piece of scenery from Grand Opera in the valley of the Skell near Ripon.

Elgar's beloved Malvern Hills formed an impressive viewpoint from which to watch rays of sunlight playing like spotlights over the fields and orchards of Worcestershire. He was impressed by their northern counterparts—by Ingleborough, standing on its platform of limestone, its gritstone cap tickling the clouds at over 2,000 feet, though if he climbed the hill no record exists in fifty years of correspondence with Buck.

It is a pity there was not enough time for him to explore that other great feature of the Yorkshire Dales—the vast tracts of heather moor in between the well-known valleys of Swale, Ure, Wharfe and Nidd.

Elgar composed some appealing music while staying at Giggleswick (or Giggleswyke, as he sometime wrote after signing a score). I mentioned some pieces in my book *Mr Elgar and Dr Buck*, published in 1991, and among them was *Rosemary*, a piece which had a modern airing in the Dales when the Librarian of Settle Orchestra came across a set of parts in the library and, having read my book, Arthur Butterworth, the conductor, decided that this little piece should be played. And so it was, at a concert held in the Ingleton Community Centre. The audience was delighted when Arthur related the story behind it.

Our conception of the Yorkshire Dales changed after the 1939-45 war, with the establishment of a National Park for the upper reaches of the major dales which extend like the fingers of a great hand from the Plain of York. The Park also takes in the slaty Howgills of the north-west but, unaccountably, does not embrace the deep trough of the upper Nidd, which is "as Dales as they mak 'em."

The dale-country is austere but attractive, with bare sheep ridges and valleys given a U-shape by glacial action, each valley having a watercourse which is cool and clear, flowing under bridges near stone-clad villages which look half as old as time. Are the people musical?

Harry Scott, who founded *The Dalesman* magazine, wrote: ''Travel where you will in our dales and moorland areas and you will get little hint of any deep-centred interest in music. . .but give the people *The Messiah* or some of the other popular oratorios, like *The Creation* or *Elijah;* give them a brass band playing *Ilkla Moor* or the hymn tune *Deep Harmony;* give them a good tune, well sung or rendered, and you have found a way to their hearts.''

Is there a distinctive Dales sound? Though we did not realise it at the time, a musical era was ending in the 1960s with the 'fiddling' of the likes of Jackie Beresford. In the days when Major Horner presided over the White Lion at Cray, Jackie arrived late, played traditional strains on his fiddle until the wee small hours, then went home for a few hours' sleep before picking up schoolchildren in his taxi and taking them to their lessons. The music of such men died with them. Their sort of pub music survives now only in the western parts of Ireland and Scotland.

Harry Scott added that while Yorkshire has many literary celebrities, it has produced few original musicians or even solo performers largely because its music is a community concern. He did instance Frederick Delius as a great original. Though born in Bradford, he had the proverbial 'soft spot' for Wharfedale but his 'high hills' were those of Scandinavia and he did spend the last thirty years of his life in France.

I tend to think of Delius in his boyhood, riding a white pony across Ilkley Moor, or as a contemplative adult, still on horseback, riding with his sister Claire from her home in Bronteland to Barden Tower, in Wharfedale, where he was fascinated by tales of the Shepherd Lord Clifford.

His niece, Margaret de Vesci, told the story of Delius and his friend, the celebrated violinist, Halfdam Jebe, while staying with Claire, going for long walks on the moors and in the Dales. ''Jebe had his violin, my mother sang and Delius played his Amati violin; he would stand perfectly still listening to the moor birds and then playing what he heard.'' When Elgar, who had also plucked tunes from the air, was an old man he flew to France to spend a little time with the dying Delius, having long recognised his worth.

In some of the old woods of the Dales—woodland where trees and outcropping rocks are lagged with moss—the strains which come to mind are those of the Norwegian composer Grieg, whom Delius met during student days at Leipsig. Music by Grieg, with its northern flavour, also held a strong appeal for Cecil Slingsby, a textile man smitten by mountains, who sauntered from his home at Carleton, near Skipton, to the alpine areas.

Slingsby, the first writer to popularise Norway as a place to be visited by mountaineers, wrote to ''Herr Grieg'' (August 20, 1900) about ''your glorious old mountains'' and expressed appreciation of one ''who has so beautifully and faithfully represented by music his country's especial charms.''

Musically, the folk of the Yorkshire Dales—farmfolk in the main—were content to sing or to dance to the music of others. A blacksmith at Gunnerside wrote songs which he performed at local concerts to tunes which were popular at the time. The dance tunes collected by enthusiasts in the 1930s are lively adaptations from popular works, including nursery rhymes. Lawrence Barker, whose family have been associated with Swaledale lead-mining for generations, could not recall for me a single song which was distinctively of the mining field, nor indeed many songs about the dale in general. A Workers' Education Association class on folk music failed to reveal anything of significance other than the several well-known songs of Swaledale.

What did emerge was that there were quite a number of violinists, 'cellists and pianists in the dale at the turn of the century. And that dalesfolk have always had a lively appreciation of good tunes, especially those incorporated in hymns to be sung lustily in chapel or melodies to which one might sing or dance.

Edmund Cooper, who delved into the folklore of Swaledale, was aware of the dalesman's high regard for music, both vocal and instrumental. "A century or two ago, these talents were expressed by the men who regularly, each Sunday, brought their flutes, fiddles, clarinets, 'cellos and trombones to church or chapel to accompany the hymn and psalm singing. Each place of worship had its minstrels' gallery or platform for their accommodation."

Minstrels played in Grinton church in 1840. Among them was Adam Barker of Healaugh. *The Messiah* was performed by Reeth residents, with the help of a few outsiders, at the Wesleyan chapel in 1848. The orchestra consisted of a double bass, violins, flutes and piano. It is related that after playing for 27 years, Adam gave his bass violin to a friend, who took it into church and was told by the parson that he would not have the fiddle in the place. A violin might still be heard at Redmire in 1854, for in that year it was provided with a new string at a cost of 1s.4d. (The previous mention of a new fiddle string had been in 1829).

When Arkendale acquired a new harmonium, in the 1860s, it was very little used. A harmonium was to be described by one Methodist preacher as "an ill wind which nobody blows any good."

Arthur Percival, who had a Wensleydale childhood, heard plenty of music. His first violin came out of his Christmas stocking when he was rising five. Arthur was to recall that "it fair glissen'd wi' orange-coloured varnish." Wear and tear necessitated its replacement on subsequent Christmases. What matter if each violin, fresh from a factory in Czechoslavakia, bore a label inside: "Guaranteed Strad. Model, made in 1741"?

Harry Cockerill, a self-taught piano accordionist who played for Dales dancing for many years, and who was related to the musical Beresfords, told me about *Varso Vianna*, a dance said to be of Scandinavian origin, and scarcely performed until Harry and, in due course, Peter

Beresford re-introduced it at old-time dances.

Harry knew of two versions. He was taught the dance by Mrs Simpson, of Stalling Busk, a pianist with quite definite ideas as to the speed. This version is now generally regarded as the oldest, being fairly slow, even sedate. Elsewhere in the area, Harry told me, it was being performed 'at a gallop' and dancers were inclined to get out of breath!

The dalesfolk were quick to absorb singable or danceable music from wherever it came. Florence Foster, born and bred at Beckermonds, where the mighty river Wharfe begins with a merger of two mountain streams, was aware of a Scandinavian connection with *Varso Vianna* and wrote: "My youngest sister, on her return from Denmark in 1926, after two years in that country, brought with her a Danish dance, which she showed to my aunt. The latter then got up and gracefully performed the 'Visovianna' (I write it as it was pronounced), an old Langstrothdale dance, which she had often performed as a girl at Beckermonds. The two dances were almost identical, and there could be no doubt in the mind of anyone seeing the two performed as to their common origin."

I am much indebted to Jennifer Wallis, of Marske, who sent me the words and music of some old songs which were popular in the Dales. They included *The Yorkshire Lass,* which I had not heard of before. It was sung by the celebrated Keld Singers of upper Swaledale but, says Jennifer, "it is not heard nowadays." Jim, the eldest of the group, sang the verses. There were no written words or music and the lyrics could vary from time to time. "What I have put as verse 2 was sung as the chorus by all." Here are the words of *The Yorkshire Lass,* which would sound much better sung than said:

Kind friends, I come before you now, my happy lot to tell;
I sing in praise of a charming girl with whom in love I fell.
She comes from out of Yorkshire, her name is Emily—
My bonny little Yorkshire Lass, my own dear Emily.

Her eyes are like the little stars that shine so bright above;
Her cheeks are like the red red rose, with her I fell in love.
She's pearly teeth and golden hair, the fairest in the land—
The pride of all the country is my bonny Yorkshire Lass.

Her father keeps a little farm not very far from here;
Amongst the flowers and roses I roam, with Emily dear—
Her father, mother, sisters, with me do all agree
The pride of all the country is my own dear Emily.

To see her in the dairy, to me is quite a treat;
Her pots, her pans and milking cans they are so trim and neat.
But far the best amongst them, and far more dear to me—
My bonnie little Yorkshire Lass, my own dear Emily.

The haunting beauty of our Yorkshire Dales have attracted talented composers who were born in other places and who brought fresh minds to a contemplation of the spacious landforms and folk life. *The Archers,* a popular BBC radio series has a signature tune which is from a Dales suite by Arthur Wood, a West Riding man whose family moved to Harrogate. He was living in London when he wrote the four movements of *My Native Heath.* A modest man who is almost forgotten, even at Harrogate, the lively movement heard daily on the radio was inspired by maypole dancing at Barwick Green. Other movements relate to Knaresborough, Ilkley Tarn and Bolton Abbey.

The Dales make a strong appeal to some modern composers. Arthur Butterworth has been inspired by moorland. Sir John Manduel, composer and retired principal of the Royal Northern College of Music, lives at High Bentham, near the Three Peaks Country, with his wife, who is a distinguished pianist and teacher. David Blake, a contemporary composer and lecturer in music at York University, lives in Swaledale. Philip Wilby, another contemporary composer, is at home in Birstwith.

It is fascinating to speculate where music-making in the

Yorkshire Dales began. The sounding of a horn at dusk, an ancient occupation for men with well-developed lungs, might be considered musical. Over forty years ago, I listened as three mighty blasts on the forest horn at Bainbridge made the air around this Wensleydale village shiver. At Bainbridge, there was much less formality than I had seen in the market place at Ripon, where the hornblower dressed up for the occasion, for dalesmen do not like a lot of fuss.

At Bainbridge, Jack Metcalfe sprang into action as the sonorous notes of Big Ben began to usher in the nine o'clock news on what was then quaintly known as the wireless. He donned his workaday jacket, lifted a large horn from its hook on the wall and walked across the road to where some large stones lay embedded in the turf of the village green. Shortly afterwards, three blasts brought a responsive echo from the fells. On a still night, the sounds had been heard at places three miles away. Jack blew the horn ''from t'back end fair to Pancake Tuesday'' or, in words better understood, from Holyrood (September 28) to Shrovetide.

The affable hornblower handed the horn to me. As a member of Hawes Silver Band, Jack could reach and maintain for as long as seven seconds a note of top C. The sound I produced was like that of a bull with a stomach disorder. The noise wavered after about three seconds and ended in a low moan. Jack's performance was a good example of living history, an echo (literally) from the days of the old Forest of Wensleydale.

J Routh, who wrote one of the first guides to Wensleydale, suggested that the practice of horn-blowing might have begun with the Romans, who had a fort at Bainbridge. It is generally said that travellers in the Forest in medieval times who ran the risk of being benighted in a hostile environment, had the sound of the horn to guide them to safety. The original horn is now in the folk museum at Bolton Castle. Jack had a horn of African origin, donated to the village in 1864. (Outside the horn-blowing season, the forest horn is displayed at the Rose and Crown in Bainbridge).

We do not know if early folk found solace in music but the Augustinian canons of Bolton Priory, in Wharfedale, ended Vespers with a hymn to the Blessed Virgin, a hymn which has survived in the Bodleian Library at Oxford. When my Lord Digby visited the Cliffords of Skipton Castle, the not inconsiderable sum of £5 was expended to bring music [minstrels?] from York. Roger the Piper, who attended during the Christmas season, received 10s for his music-making.

At Barden Tower, in Wharfedale, where the Lord Clifford (1485-1524) is usually pictured as a studious recluse, shut off from the world, the accounts reveal expenditure on music and entertainment. There must have been some resident musicians for payments were made for strings for a fiddle. Young Long, the Piper, was provided with a livery jacket to be worn when he played the bagpipes. Payment was made for players from Halifax on St Thomas's day.

Bolton Priory, Wharfedale.

At Christmas, in the seventeenth century, the lodge-keepers and farmers were invited to a special gathering, and a stag was killed to provide the assembly with venison pie, baked by Widow Bland. A century later, Willie Young of Appletreewick, wearing his best swallow-tailed green coat, earned local history renown for the quality of his dancing.

17

Towards the end of the eighteenth century, Francis King, the Skipton minstrel, attended fairs and feasts despite being both blind and lame—so lame that he said that no other King ever had so many ups and downs in life. He had four fiddles, named Fanny, Betsy, Peggy and Sally. He was popular especially among the lead-miners of Grassington. Francis was drowned when, after Gargrave Feast, he strayed from the straight and narrow towpath into the canal.

William Bolton, believed to be a native of Richmond, combined a career of scissors-grinding and sharpening the cut-throat type of razor (hence his nickname Razop) with singing, fiddling and piping. On a headstone in Burnsall churchyard, in Wharfedale, he is described as The Dales Minstrel. Incidentally, he was so well regarded by dalesfolk that the headstone was erected to his memory by public subscription, despite his habit of spending a few hours getting his pipes into tune and then sallying forth to show them off.

This Dales Minstrel is mentioned in *English Poets, Ballads and Songs of the Peasantry of England* (1874). An account tells of him singing a song called *The Garden Gate,* ''one of our most pleasing ditties. The air is very beautiful. We first heard it sung Malhamdale, Yorkshire, by Willy Bolton, an old Dales-minstrel, who accompanied himself on the union pipes.''

Long since, Brass Bands and Singers went on their Christmas rounds of remote farmhouses. At Beckermonds, in Langstrothdale (and doubtless elsewhere) they were toasted with a liberal quantity of mulled air, made by William Foster, who beat up a great many fresh eggs and mixed them with warm beer. Florence Foster, writing in the 1940s, recalled one man rendering *While Shepherds* as a solo to an old tune she had not heard elsewhere. ''Possibly he had just had a pint of mulled ale from the bucket.''

Neddy Dick, of Keld, at the head of Swaledale, astonished friends and visitors by playing a 'rock instrument', fashioned from stones of various sizes picked up on the screes and painstakingly arranged to form a cumbersome forerunner of the xylophone. Neddy's real name was Richard William Alderson. Tall, thin and a bachelor, Neddy lived by himself and was a self-taught musician whose pride and joy was his *orgin* (harmonium) until, dissatisfied with the doleful sound he thought it would be much improved by the addition of bells.

Neddy cut down an apple tree, trimming it so as to form a base which he attached to the harmonium with two branches, one above another, thus extending the length of the harmonium. Neddy then attached clock bells to the branches and somehow managed to tune them so that he might play the harmonium with one hand and hit the bells with the other hand. To obtain his set of bells, he travelled miles to hear striking clocks. If one had a bell of a suitable weight and pitch, he would buy or exchange it with one in his collection.

When ringing the bells palled, he turned to the limestone clints, bearing large stones from near Kisdon Force, tuning them by knocking off pieces from either side or the ends to make a piece either sharp or flat. He then mounted his stones on trestles. They were a great success, as will be related.

Some of the Dales market towns have maintained a tradition for staging light opera, the productions of Gilbert and Sullivan being popular until the wave of modern productions, in some of which Dalesfolk were called upon to adopt the American drawl. Settle Amateurs have performed in the Victoria Hall, which still has something of the flavour of the old-time music hall, for over a century. When Hawes Operatic Amateurs staged *Ruddigore* in 1931, they had three venues on successive evenings, these being Hawes, Leyburn and Kirkby Stephen.

Could the pot cuckoos of Pateley Bridge be regarded as musical? A gipsy stayed overnight at the Royal Oak. Not having the money to pay his bill, he left two china cuckoos with the landlord in settlement. The 'birds' were subsequently used to initiate newcomers into the fraternity of the inn.

'Tis true my love has list - ed, he wears a white cock-ade; He is a hand-some young man be - side a ro - ving blade. He is a hand-some young man, and he's gone to serve the King, O my ver - y, O my ver - y; O my ver - y, O my ver - y My ver - y heart is break - ing, all for the love of him.

"The White Cockade," which was heard at West Witton.

One of the cuckoos produced a long and plaintive note when blown into and the other covered the blower with a cloud of white flour. Originally, soot was used. So famous did the birds become it was said you might distinguish the true Nidderdale man by asking him if he had seen the cuckoos.

The old-time dances held today contain steps devised in quite recent times. The true old-time dances were becoming a memory towards the end of the 1930s. One person dates the decline from the celebration of the Coronation of George V, when old and young celebrated together. By this time, the old-time isolation of the Dales was breaking down as transport improved, the dalesfolk could go further without much effort, and the wireless was relaying news and entertainment of the outside world.

The Dales, especially Wensleydale, with its castles at Bolton and Middleham, is still capable of putting on a show based on historic associations. Such was the Bolton Castle Festival, held in the summer of 1951, when the old building was repeopled as it might have been in the Elizabethan period and the signal that the Scrope family (motto—'forward, if I can') was 'in residence' was the flag flying from the ramparts. Its pennant, fourteen feet long, had been painted by Fred Lawson, a famous local artist.

Musically, there was country dancing to a melodeon. The dance teams came from Bellerby and Leyburn. In the evening, the Wensleydale Choir rendered excerpts from *Merrie England*, followed by *Jerusalem* and the National Anthem. At Middleham, the old-time flavour has been captured by productions under the auspices of English Heritage.

I completed my inquiry into Dales music with a feeling that much remains to be re-discovered—that in cupboards and attics of many a dales home there must be records of folk song and music which would deserve to be heard again.

Do any copies remain of the gramophone record issued in 1963 by the Huddlestons of Rectory Farm, Rillington—a record of Yorkshire songs, three of them from the north-east coast and one, *The White Cockade,* heard at the Burning of Bartle ceremony at West Witton, in Wensleydale, and recorded by a group of singers at Redmire? Profits from the sale of the record were to be given to the National Folk Music Fund.

And what has happened to the score of the *Askrigg Concerto*? It was reported in *The Dalesman* of 1943 to have been written by John Crowther, a Yorkshire-born musician and composer and member of the BBC Theatre Orchestra. While on a fishing holiday, staying at the Wensleydale village of Askrigg, he collected Wensleydale folk-tunes and arranged and scored them for performance by a string orchestra. He found a sympathetic spirit in the person of R M Chapman, a native of Askrigg who became a schoolteacher at Shipley but returned to the Dales at every opportunity.

It was 'Dick' Chapman who put forward the idea of an *Askrigg Concerto*. The composer had his day's fishing, then returned to Yoredale House to find his host, Mr Weatherall, whistling tunes over to him. Dick Chapman organised a family gathering at Mill Farm and further tunes were played over. The rhythm of one of them was tapped out to make quite sure that the composer had noted it fully. The correct melodic progress of one tune could not be recalled correctly until Dick rang up another relative who, unabashed, sang the tune over the telephone. More telephoning. Themes were whistled, hummed, played, tapped out—and this in wartime, when telephone operators must have suspected Fifth Column activity.

When the feverish activity had ended, Crowther had the nucleus of a musical work, but not enough for a concerto. Mention is made of the composing of a *Yorkshire Suite* for String Orchestra called Wensleydale, in the following movements: 1) Minuet. Aysgarth—by the Falls. 2) A Prayer. Askrigg Church. 3) Gavotte. Bainbridge. On the Village Green. 4) Hornpipe. Hawes—Fair Day. It was played over locally but where—oh where—has the score gone?

The rarefied art of the avant-garde has been inspired by the sheep farming traditions of the Yorkshire Dales in the television opera, transmitted in 1987, called *Yan Tan Tethera,* the composer being Harrison Birtwistle of Accrington. Stan Roocroft, a former musical advisory teacher for Sheffield, who lives in Hawes, has been at the hub of directing the local operatic society and brass band, though he would be the first to acknowledge the enthusiastic efforts of many local people. Swaledale Festival, held every two years, produces a regular upsurge in musical activity.

Music and drama still feature strongly in the life of Scargill House, a conference and holiday centre near Kettlewell, where many people draw away from the busy world to reflect in natural surroundings. The chapel of Scargill House, venue for regular services and of many outstanding musical performances, impresses by its bold triangular shape and the size of the main timbers, fashioned from Columbian pine, sweeping upwards like human hands in the attitude of prayer. Or perhaps they are like the spars of a nordic ship, appropriate to an upper dale which was settled, a thousand years and more ago, by people with a Scandinavian ancestry.

It was here, in a structure which took shape less than forty years ago, that I reflected generally on the subject of Music in the Yorkshire Dales. My thoughts ranged from medieval minstrels to the grand concerts of modern times, when an influx of retired folk has been a stimulus to all kinds of social activity. Not long before, this chapel of Scargill House had been packed by patrons attending a concert in a programme devised for the Grassington Festival.

Now, under a vast cedar-shingle roof, looking at the Dales through Alpine-style gable ends which are mainly of glass, I temporarily had the place to myself and could let my mind fill with glorious strains.

Christmas in the Dale

Words and music by Mike Donald

The Three Peaks in the sky Like Shep-herds old and wise In the half light of the ever lone — ly star That spark-les in the Gill and the mel-an-cho-ly mill and once again it's Christ-mas in the Dale Frozen Mill and snow capp'd hill waitin for the mail once again It's Christ-mas In the Dale

The Dales In Song

IN DALES dialect, the words themselves seem to sing. The songs, reflecting local pride, with a mention of well-known characters, were meant to be sung to jaunty tunes, many of which have now been lost, though in recent times, when a bus party of old Swaledale residents was returning home from a day out, someone struck up a song which begins "I've a lile bit of hay left on my baulks," one of several compositions by William Calvert, the blacksmith at Gunnerside.

The Dales had their Singers, small groups of dalesfolk who sang in their own districts the ballads especially associated with them or sacred songs which appealed in particular to the large chapel-going public. The Garsdale Singers, active from 1936 until 1966, included five of the thirteen children of Roland and Mary Jane Bracken.

The Keld Singers earned wide renown because, in the 1930s, they were invited to sing before the microphone in the Leeds studio of the BBC. Two surviving members, Laurie Rukin and Chris Alderson, who appeared in a television series entitled *A Dales Diary*, were interviewed to a 'backing' provided by unaccompanied singing of an old song, *Lily Dale*, which once was part of the Keld Singers' repertoire.

The present Swaledale Singers keep alive the tradition of vocal music in the district. Jennifer Wallis, of Gingle Pot Farm, Marske, a member of the group (as is her husband George) sorted out the Swaledale songs for me and performed a great duty to Dales music by writing out the music as she remembers it. Two songs were rendered, one being *Beautiful Swaledale* (Land of Rest), which is "amusing, lively, bouncy and is delivered in broad Yorkshire dialect, NEVER in chapels or churches." The other, *Beautiful Dale* (Home of the Swale), was sung in sacred concerts, being more refined.

A well-loved clergyman in Malhamdale was sent on his way into retirement on the crest of a musical wave. The last Sunday in the Ministry of the Rev Barry Newth, July 20, 1997, was to be memorable when the evening service was devoted to the singing of popular hymns by a large congregation, plus the Giggleswick and Settle Band and the Malhamdale Choir.

Songs of Swaledale

The old songs have lingered in the minds of a few songsters who have performed them at concerts or chapel occasions. Even now, it does not take long to persuade Laurie Rukin or Chris Alderson to sing a few lines of the song *Beautiful Swaledale*, which has been recorded in recent times, the dalesmen having memorised it, singing the celebrated piece sometimes in unison and sometimes as a solo and often with Laurie vamping on the piano. Sometimes, the verses were sung by individuals following a discussion on stage (to the amusement of the audience) about how the singing should be allocated, verse by verse. The rest of the quartette joined in the chorus in harmony.

The first time I heard the song was in the autumn of 1952. I had completed a long and tedious series of bus journeys from Ribblesdale into Swaledale and set about collecting information to be incorporated in *Dalesman* articles. I began the first piece with the chorus of *Beautiful Swaledale*.

> Beautiful Swaledale, land of rest;
> Beautiful Swaledale, I love thee the best.
> The land it is set in a cultivate style:
> The extension of Swaledale is twenty long mile.

Twenty long mile! A rambler I met near Muker said that until he set out to walk up the dale he had not realised how long those miles really are. "Anyway," he added, "it was only my feet that complained. The road up Swaledale is one of the hardest I have ever trod. The rest of me thoroughly enjoyed the trip. You know, Swaledale is wonderfully compact. The hills are never so far apart that you feel you are missing anything.''

He loved the purple moors about Reeth and the sweep of the fells higher up. He found the villages exciting. "And the folk! They all have a pride in the dale and a community sense. I suppose their homeliness has been brought about by their isolation." Indeed. I had not been in Swaledale half an hour before someone referred warmly to 't'dale' and spoke of a resident at the top end as though that person only lived at the end of the street. On the other hand, Mrs Nancy Parker who presided over the Post Office at Muker had been born at the nearby village of Gunnerside. She had lived in Muker since 1912 but was still thought of as a 'Gunnersider' by t'older end!

It has been claimed that the best-known Swaledale ballad was written by Mark Ralph Peacock, who was born in the valley last century and spent most of his life at Low Row, between Gunnerside and Reeth, at a time when a daily sight was that of lead-miners plodding to their work at the local mines, notably Old Gang, tucked away in a heather-girt valley out of sight of the main dale.

Swaledale is the favourite dale of many people because it is small and therefore comprehensible. It also appears to be in a time-warp, but change is in the nature of Swaledale. As I write, a conspicuous building Gunnerside Lodge, formerly the home of Lord Peel, is in process of being extended. In Victorian times, men earned a chancy living from mining and women remained at home to look after the many children and to attend to the work on the few fields and small barn which passed for a farm at the dalehead. Within living memory, dozens of such smallholdings have been amalgamated to form viable farms on which sheep and beef cattle are kept.

As the chorus of the old ballad declares, Swaledale is

beautiful—a sliver of green between the lean landscape of the moors, with Kisdon, the 'island hill', standing out prominently near Muker. One of the glories of the dale today is formed of the meadowland, much of which has not been given the modern treatment, which transforms a floriferous vegetation into the uniform green of a rye-grass mix, suited for big-bag silage making. Photographers usually make for a roadside vantage point east of Gunnerside to capture on film the broad, flat valley with its pattern of drystone walls and many little field barns.

Though Mark Peacock has been mentioned as the author of the ballad, the lyrics are uneven, implying that they—like Swaledale itself—has been subject to change. The Song of one man became a community effort. It is not especially good poetry, but to the dalesfolk who have grown up with it, the *Song of Swaledale* is an expression of their deep love for the place.

The first time I heard the chorus of the ballad sung, I was sitting with Laurie Rukin at the fireside of his home at Keld, near the head of the dale. His father, Jack, was postman for thirty years, his round including the hostelry on Tan Hill. Laurie is one of two surviving members of the group known as the Keld Singers, being a nephew of three Alderson brothers—Chris (known as Kitty and still alive and alert, as already mentioned), James (Mosser) and Richard (Dick).

When they sang on t'wireless in the 1930s, their local fame was confirmed. They were transported, along with a celebrated character, Susan Peacock, of Tan Hill Inn, and did not show too many nerves when they were arranged around the microphone in a well-lagged studio. Susan was a lover of 'quiet places' and afterwards remarked that t'wireless did not appeal to her, and that her husband, Michael, ''is not struck on it either.''

Dick Guy, who was well-known in Swaledale as a singer and concert artiste, described the Singers to me as ''just ordinary farm lads who sing of their native dale and also render North Country ballads. The only practice they get is while singing to the cows and sheep while going about their work.'' Dick was a member of the Muker Quartet Party, the other three members being Mr and Mrs Tom Parker and Mrs Maggie Fawcett.

Vocal groups proliferated in the pre-television dale-country. The Swaledale Veteran's Choir was open to anyone over seventy years of age. When the Choir took part in a broadcast it was headed by George Alderson, the shoemaker at Gunnerside, who was then eighty-three years old. George was over ninety when he died. Cotty (Henry Cottingham), a keen songster, was fond of rendering a doleful ditty concerning age and death which profoundly affected his audience and at the same time tickled his sense of humour. It began:

> Cotty's journey to the grave is short,
> > His work is almost done;
> His tottering limbs grow weaker,
> > His race is nearly run.

As noted, *Beautiful Swaledale* (Land of Rest) was sung by Laurie and Chris for Yorkshire Television. On the most recent occasion I have chatted with Laurie, it was not in his home at Keld, the setting for so many of our conversations but at St John's Methodist Chapel at Settle, to which he was taken by relatives he was visiting in North Ribblesdale. It was good to hear a Swaledale voice lifted in praise during the singing of some old familiar hymns. Mike Porter has several times recorded Laurie, despite his protestations that his voice had faded somewhat. His melodic voice is heard in Mike's video, aptly named 'Beautiful Swaledale', which emphasises folk activity as well as glorious scenery.

Here is one version of *Beautiful Swaledale*:

> There's Law Raw and Feetham stands near to the Swale.
> They're two of the best places we have in the Dale.
> For owt ye can mention, it doesn't matter what,
> There isn't yan in 'em that cares for the cat.

Beautiful Swaledale (LAND OF REST)

1. Beautiful Swaledale land of my birth, Beautiful Swaledale, 'tis not known thy worth, Thy cattle and sheep and grass on the moors, and pigs made of lead bring in money like showers.

Chorus.
Beautiful Swaledale land of rest, Beautiful Swaledale I love thee the best. The land it is set in a cultivale style, the extention of Swaledale is twenty long mile

Chorus:
> Beautiful Swaledale, the land of rest,
> Beautiful Swaledale, I love thee the best,
> The land, it is set in a cultivate style.
> The extent of Swaledale is twenty long mile.

There's twa or three misers, that I'll allow
Who are studying to save money to as low as mi shoe.
They keep all their brass in an aud stocking leg.
The next thing you'll hear 'em starting to beg.

There's Ivelet and Satron and Coverdy House,
There isn't yan in 'em that's worth a louse.
For the shepherds' feast nobbut comes yance a year,
And they tak' good care to get their share of beer.

There's Muker an Waite, twa ancient toons,
For seeing auld wommin wearing bedgowns.
They're nearly all farmers and live on their own grounds,
And in Hawes bank they've got plenty of pounds.

There's Angram and Thorns a bit farther up,
And all that they are good for is getting out muck.
They're sitting in t'nuke and smoking all t'time,
While the auld benty pastures is wanting some lime.

Away farther up on Blackmoor Fell
Some jolly auld farmers here do well,
Who never sees nowt, but their own house riggin',
And live five mile from their own middin.

Here are the words of *Beautiful Dale* (Home of the Swale). As words alone they might seem ordinary, but allied to the music and in the emotion of a major chapel occasion they bring a tear to many a Swaledale eye.

> I sing of a place to my heart very dear
> A place where I always will dwell
> And if you will kindly lend me your ear
> A few of its beauties I'll tell.

Beautiful Dale (HOME OF THE SWALE)

Chorus:
  In that beautiful dale, home of the Swale
  How well do I love thee, how well (do I love thee)
  Beautiful dale, home of the Swale
  Beautiful, beautiful dale.

Tis far, far away from the noise and the din
Of collieries and factories and mills
From the bustle and strife of town life shut in
By verdant and radiant hills.

Home often as boys have we wandered along
By the side of that river so clear;
The birds never fail to trill their sweet song
And lend a charm to our ear.

Oh Swaledale, Sweet Dale, thou closely art bound
To our hearts by the strongest of ties
That ever in human hearts can be found
The sources of our greatest joys.

And if fate compels me to leave the dear spot
And in other lands far away roam;
My earnest wish, what ere be my lot
Is to end my days here at home.

Jennifer Wallis heard *Beautiful Swaledale* being rendered by vocalists living at Dungworth, near Sheffield. She had switched on the television as she cooked the Sunday dinner on December 8, 1996. Gloria Hunniford, on *Sunday Live*, introduced a feature on old Christmas carols and Jennifer was reminded by their informality and gusto of the present Swaledale Singers, of which she and her husband are members.

Mention of Dungworth, near Sheffield, puzzled her. "This was our song, unique to Swaledale. How was it that people from another part of the county were singing it, using the same words and tune, and singing it with obvious love and enjoyment?" Thrilled to hear the song on national television, but baffled as to how it came to be included in a feature on Christmas carols, she wrote to Yorkshire Television. ''They wrote back, thanking me for my interest and saying they were passing my letter to Ian Russell, Director of *Village Carols*, who would be able to answer my question about Swaledale.''

Ian Russell promptly replied, stating that Albert and Bernard Broadhead, two keen ramblers and carollers from the Sheffield area, used to visit the Dales regularly from the 1940s to the 1970s. ''They had a very dear friend who lived near Gunnerside called Edgar Tissiman, who died about 1973. He was one of the first National Park wardens in the Dales. In his company, they learnt the song at the local pub...Back in Sheffield, the brothers would perform it as their party piece and it has since become very popular. Bernard died about 1975.

''Because there is nowadays so very little singing apart from Christmas, Albert would be asked to sing the song as part of the Christmas carolling. Thus people came to associate it with Christmas. Billy Mills, the farmer who sang it on the TV clip, learnt the song from Albert, who died last year (1996) in his 91st year. Billy now performs the song at the Royal Hotel, Dungworth, every Sunday in the six weeks up to Christmas and everyone loves it...The Dungworth carolling (and *Swaledale*) is featured on a recording published for Christmas 1996.''

There were echoes of the famous song when a Western Dales Young Farmers' Club Rally took place in 1993. Among the competitive classes was one for devising a county anthem, to be performed by any number of members, with or without instruments. An anthem was hurriedly composed as an entry by the Reeth YFC and set to the tune of *Beautiful Dale*. There was extra incentive to do well because a similar class appeared in the schedule of the Yorkshire YFC rally, to be held at Harrogate.

The Western Dales district comprises three clubs—Reeth,

Lily Dale

Lower Wensleydale and Masham—so, with points and trophies at stake, the Wallis family of Gingle Pot, Marske, set about making up a Yorkshire anthem in rollicking YFC style. Those involved were George and Jennifer, Martin and Brenda. At the rally, Martin and Brenda, Rachel Porter and Philip Stones, plus anyone not otherwise occupied in stock-judging, flower arranging or log-sawing, wore check-pattern shirts, work trousers held up with braces, and flat caps. They were awarded the first prize.

The song was polished up for the County Rally, a day to remember, with Rachel Porter rushing to change out of her dressmaking and modelling outfit and Martin Wallis rushing between the sheep shearing and town crier classes. Their reward, as before, was first prize. In 1997, a class for a County Anthem appeared again and the words of the Swaledale entry were found and dusted down. The famous tune was taught to junior members and the entry gained first prize at the Western Dales Rally, second place at Harrogate and third at the Northern Area Rally held at Durham.

Among the verses which illustrate the adaptability of dalesfolk to new ideas was:

> Our Yorkshire Pudding and Wensleydale Cheese
> For flavour and taste are renowned;
> John Smiths and Theakstons, two pints that will please
> Are certainly the best to be found.

Lily Dale

When *A Dales Dairy*, produced by Yorkshire Television, included an interview with Laurie Rukin and Chris Alderson, a tape of the Keld Singers was borrowed and used as background music. The selected piece was a desperately sad but tuneful ditty called *Lily Dale*, unaccompanied, with a typical close harmonius sound of Dales voices which blended well. *Lily Dale* had often been sung in the northern valleys of what is now the Yorkshire Dales National Park. The third verse was always omitted, possibly because it would have reduced everyone to tears.

'Twas a calm still night and the moon's pale light
Shone soft o'er hill and vale,
When friends mute with grief stood around the death bed
Of my poor lost Lily Dale.

Chorus (softly):
    O Lily, sweet Lily, dear Lily Dale
    Now the wild rose blossoms o'er her little green grave
    Neath the trees in the flowery dale.

Her cheeks that once glowed with the rose tint of health
By the hand of disease had turned pale
And the death damp was on the pure white brow
Of my poor lost Lily Dale.

I go, she said, to the land of rest
And 'ere my strength shall fail—
I must tell you where near my own loved home
You must lay poor Lily Dale.

Neath the chestnut tree where the wild flowers grow
And the stream ripples forth through the vale
Where the birds shall warble their songs in spring
There lay poor Lily Dale.

The Singing Blacksmith

The history of Gunnerside smithy is interwoven with that of Swaledale to the extent that it was thriving with the lead mines and has provided a service for local farmers since the 1840s. David, James, William and Jim were the Calverts who laboured long and hard in a smithy where bellows were hand-operated and shoes shaped by t'rack o' t'eye.

The first time I called at t'awd smiddy, just before haytime in 1952, a welcome was extended by Willie Calvert, who told me that with his son, Jim, he had shod fourteen horses in a single day. The farms were slowly being mechanised but the horse—mainly t'Dales gallowa' (galloway)—was still needed where the slopes were so severe the farm folk would have benefited from having one leg shorter than the other.

Willie Calvert had the smithy at Gunnerside and, on Wednesday, travelled updale to man that at Thwaite. He also did a bit of farming and when hand-milking the cattle he made up songs, to be sung at local concerts, using popular tunes of the day. Willie's lyrics were hugely entertaining, but his singing was not of the best, with the result that the accompanist on the piano would sometimes stop so they might get the rendition sorted out. The banter between the two was in itself amusing. He entertained in concerts at various places in the dale, including Muker.

His son, Jim, reminded me that local concerts were the main sources of entertainment before wireless and television were developed. "In other words, they made their own entertainment." The village hall at Gunnerside was built in 1870, when the area held a large number of miners.

I was permitted to use this transcript of the tape-recording of a dialect song, *Farming Up in Swaledale*, which was written by William Calvert and sung by his grandson, Stephen Calvert, in 1973:

Oh, I'se farmin' up i' Swodill (Swaledale)
   and I'se gitten short o' hay,
This storm has maed a mess o' me
   In ivvery sort o' way—
For when I started winter
I thought I'd hev hay to spar
But now it's nearly finished, and I'll hetta late (look for)
   some mar (more).

Chorus:

Oh, I've fothered (fed) me yows and I've fothered me cow
But this weean't last se lang,
And a bit o' brass that I heve seaved
   It'll all ga wi' a bang.
Me neighbours keep on assen (asking) me
And me wife she fairly talks—
For to tell y'ot truth all t'hay I've left
Is a lile bit on the boax (hay loft).

Now when I ga to sleep at neight, I dream of nowt but hay—
And oft I lewk at t'Almanac and count up days till May,
But it'll be a bit afore, the grass begins to sprout.
Oh—how I wish that I could sit and hear the cuckoo shout.

Oh what a braal (bawl) the cows all give when I turn out
   each day;
Their tongues are hingin' fra' their mouths
All waitin' for their hay.
I put 'em all on rations now but this waean't last se lang,
I give them all a nice lile bit and shut the dewer (door)
   and run.

Mining families who had left the dale to find employment in the North East or the textile belt of Lancashire returned to Gunnerside for the Midsummer Festival in the large Methodist Chapel. The pews were inadequate to hold all the people and chairs had to be placed in the aisles. The hymn-singing was vibrant and the tunes *Gunnerside* and *Muker*, composed by James Reynoldson, were favourites.

The Song of Upper Wharfedale

This is the work of a single hand, that of William Foster of Beckermonds, a scattering of buildings at the head of Langstrothdale. Austere but attractive, the little valley, rimmed by limestone, is the nursery of the river Wharfe. The church at Hubberholme is renowned for its rood loft, a survival of medieval days. Just across the river bridge stands the George Inn, once the property of the benefice and the setting for an annual Land Letting, an occasion for much talk, drinking and song. The land annually offered for rent is the Poor Pasture, the proceeds originally benefiting the poor of the parish.

In *The Dales Song*, the link with a traditional local ballad comes with the proud declaration:

> Beautiful Wharfedale so sweet and so fair,
> Nowhere in England can with thee compare.

Mr Foster, a big man, six foot high and broadly built, was famed for his feats of physical strength as well as for his ability to make words sing. When he composed the *Song of Upper Wharfedale*, to a traditional air, he doubtless had his cousin, Alan Beresford, in mind, he being a member of the Langstrothdale String Band. The score does not appear to have been recorded, though as recently as the 1940s several old people in the area were said to recall it. Sing it to whatever tune will fit!.

The words of the Song, which traces Langstrothdale from the 'top house' to where it joins Wharfedale proper, were eventually published in the *Craven Herald*. Again, the poetry is not outstanding but the work gives the flavour of Dales life in the middle of last century:

Hubberholme

Foremost and first of High Greenfield I'll tell,
Where you'll find Jeffrey and Ninian as well.
Jeff is renowned for the pigeons he's shot,
Ninian is known for the photos he's got.

Low Greenfield I'll sing, with its grand shooting-box,
Its weather-cock swinging—I think it's a fox.
Albert is coachman and butler as well,
While Ned rears the stock for John Gill to sell.

Beckermonds comes next in the valley so low,
There you'll find Foster and Beresford also.
Foster's a man with a heart for the grouse,
Beresford sings a good song in Lodge House.

Let's call at George Beresford's, up at Cowside,
Hen-keeping and making great pigs is his pride.
He holds the New House, but he doesn't there stay,
Nothing lives there but a ghost, as folks say.

Deepdale comes next at the foot of Sty Gill,
With Peacock and Rowland and Ottie and Will.
Peacock has fame for the lambs he could raise,
Ottie's a horse-judge that all men can praise.

41

Turnbull is next, and he keeps a shop,
Nothing he's short of—from needle to pop.
Granny is cosy juist in the next street,
A nicer old lady no one can meet.

Look how Willie Thwaite can live at his ease,
With winning such prizes for butter and cheese.
Margaret knits on in her neat little cot,
Chapman and Wyle make up a good lot.

Netherghyll comes next, but no one lives there,
So Frank minds the stock with very great care.
Swarthghyll is bonny and cannot be dull,
They caught the big fish, and tried to kill t'bull.

Cam Houses are yonder, up the hillside,
Sander and Alick and Bob there reside.
Beautiful Wharfedale, so sweet and so fair,
Nowhere in England can with thee compare.

At Yockenthwaite dwelling with pick and with spade,
Old George for a long time our good roads has made.
Beresford John, with his gun he goes out,
While Lodge, Tom and Auty, are somewhere about.

Raisgill's the next stop just over the green,
Captain's good bottle can often be seen.
Ottiwell's gone over there to reside,
And brought his fair wife to live by his side.

Grace Pawson's the next, she keeps the George Inn,
Many a good dalesman kens t'taste of her gin.
Hard by lives the Parson, he's very good,
While Edmund Dixon's snug under the wood.

Ben Lofthouse loves Cray and his 'White Lion Inn'.
While his grand trotting horse the prizes does win.
Robinson's out on his land near and far,
It's there you'll find Dick Hill, Lambert and Sahr.

Now back we return to Oughtershaw Hall,
It's fir trees, flowers and grand waterfall.
Look in at the School and you'll see Mr Simms,
Teaching bairns songs, recitations and hymns.

Sweet lass of Rich-mond Hill! Sweet lass of Rich-mond Hill! I'd crowns re-sign To call her mine; Sweet lass of Rich-mond Hill!

D.S.

The Lass of Richmond Hill

Richmond, by the Swale, is associated with an early Dales percussionist—a little Drummer Boy, who is said to walk backwards and forwards in a tunnel between Richmond Castle and Easby Abbey. Much better known is the poem which became a love song about a Sweet Lass who lived on Richmond Hill.

The poem was written by Leonard MacNally, an Irish dramatist and barrister. He fell in love with Frances I'Anson, or Janson, who is associated in popular legend with Hill House (then known simply as The Hill), which stands at the top of Frenchgate in Richmond, Yorkshire. Down the years, at least seven names have been canvassed as the original Lass and the setting for the song has alternated with Richmond, Surrey. At the time of writing, to the chagrin of Yorkshire folk, the claims of Surrey are favoured.

43

Richmond, Yorkshire, is an attractive old town clustering round a Norman castle. Georgian buildings overlook a cobbled market place. Streets of picturesque houses radiate from this central feature, seeming (to unquestioning people, which means most of us) to be an ideal setting for the heart-rending ballad about the Sweet Lass. Leslie P Wenham, a local historian, after observing that the story of the Lass being wooed and won by Leonard MacNally in the garden of the Hill House is a cardinal principal of faith to most north-countrymen, went on to demolish it.

I recall with what vehemence the Yorkshire link was asserted by readers of *The Dalesman* when it was suggested that the Lass was none other than Mrs Fitzherbert, the wife of the Prince Regent (later George IV). Leslie, tirelessly and impartially investigating the romantic theme of Frances and Leonard, found very little of the story stood up to close scrutiny. If you prefer the old romantic tale, read no further.

Leonard is said to have written his love letter while reclining in the shade of a walnut tree in the garden of Hill House, a pretty but unlikely idea, as is the claim that Frances was banished from London to Richmond, Yorkshire, because of her friendship with MacNally. She never lived at Hill House, though there was a family connection. Here for some twelve years before her marriage lived the young lady who was to become the mother of the Sweet Lass.

Frances I'Anson, who most people agree was the beauty MacNally had in mind when he wrote his ballad, was the fourth of five children of William I'Anson and Martha (nee Hutchinson). Leslie Wenham's researches indicate she was born in Leyburn on October 17, 1766 and baptised in Wensley Church on November 11 of that same year. At Leyburn, anyone who goes to Richmond via Bellerby has the long haul up 'Richmond hill'.

The I'Ansons left Leyburn in 1773 and her father was later recorded as being a lawyer, with a house in Bedford Row, London. It was presumably here, where soirees and other social functions took place, that Frances first met Leonard MacNally, at a time when he was a celebrity for his opera *Robin Hood*. Mr and Mrs I'Anson found the friendship distasteful, but despite the wishes of her father that it might be brought to an end Frances married the dashing Irishman, the ceremony taking place at St George's, Hanover Square, in 1787. She was promptly disinherited.

Against the odds, the marriage was happy. A letter from MacNally to his brother-in-law noted: "Seven years have now nearly elapsed since our marriage, and though we have experienced some severe rubs, I can say for her as I can sincerely say of myself, there has not been a moment of repentance..." As to the song, which is one of the most romantic love letters ever set to music, MacNally's name was not associated with it as author when it was first published in the *Morning Post and Daily Advertiser* of August 1, 1789. He had written lots of poems and other work. The simple but heartfelt little ballad might have remained obscure but for James Hook, a popular composer of the day, who set it to music. To Hook, it was just one of some 2,000 tunes he wrote down. None of the others has been remembered.

Was Frances in the large company who heard *Sweet Lass of Richmond Hill* being sung for the first time at Vauxhall Gardens? Almost certainly. Charles Benjamin Incledon, a noted tenor, first rendered what was to become an eighteenth century 'top of the pops'. The soloist had the 'backing' of violins, flutes and horns. So successful was his rendering of the song that he was engaged to perform at Covent Garden Opera House.

According to Wenham's researches, Frances gave birth to at least five children, two of whom—Frances and Elisabeth—outlived her. Leonard and Frances spent the first five years of her marriage in London and the last three in Dublin.

Here are the words of The Lass of Richmond Hill:

On Richmond Hill there lived a lass,
More sweet than May-day morn,
Whose charms all other maids surpass,
A rose without a thorn.
This lass so neat,
With smile so sweet,
Has won by right good will,
I'd crowns resign to call her mine,
Sweet lass of Richmond Hill.

Ye zephyrs fair that fan the air,
And wanton thro' the grove,
Oh! whisper to my charming fair,
"I die for her I love."
This lass so neat, &c.

How happy will the shepherd be,
Who calls his maid his own;
Oh! may her choice be fixed on me,
Mine's fixed on her alone.
This lass so neat, &c.

The romance between the young couple was touched with tragedy, and she died in Dublin on September 20, 1795, at the early age of twenty-nine. Soon after the death of his wife, Leonard McNally moved from London to his native Dublin, where he is believed to have combined a successful legal practice with sinister activity as a secret agent for the government. He joined some Irish conspiracies and betrayed his associates, for a price.

Part of the walnut tree from the Hill House garden was preserved and, in 1944, built into the fireplace of the Town Clerk's Lodging in Frenchgate. Richmond Corporation named two new roads—I'Anson Road and Frances Road—in honour of the Sweet Lass of Richmond Hill.

Music for Dancing

AT Askrigg Fair, held in June, an "old-fashioned merry dance" was performed. It was said to be going out of fashion in the 1840s. At Muker, in Swaledale, where Awd Roy was celebrated on the Wednesday before Old Christmas Day (January 6), there was dancing by candlelight from about six o'clock in an upper room of the Queen's Head. Marie Hartley and Joan Ingilby have recorded that the first dance, known as the Stot, was performed by men only. A favourite dance was the *Wensleydale Gallop*, which was a kind of *Sir Roger de Coverley*. Everyone joined in.

The grand finale, on the Saturday night, was the 'whishin' or cushion dance, which originated in the days of Good Queen Bess. "Everyone was seated round the room and when the fiddlers struck up a lovely air, a young man led off by bringing a cushion and placing it before his favourite girl. They knelt and kissed. A girl then laid the cushion before her choice and so it went on until all had found partners. If anyone refused to kneel they were gently pushed down with a brush."

The couples finally joined arms and tripped round the room, singing:

> Arm in arm, round and round,
> Me that loves a bonny lass
> Will kiss her on the ground.

Much of the old-time music of the Dales survived because people danced to it and, although in many cases they were not written down, the strains were rendered fluently by the fiddlers or players of the melodeon who provided the musical accompaniment at informal dances, held in the flagged kitchens of old farmhouses or in outbuildings when, at farms where sheep-clipping took place with a greatly augmented labour force, the day ended with a good meal and dancing well into the night. In some cases, a dancer who walked home arrived there just in time to change his clothes and start the morning milking.

Florence Foster, who recorded her memories of Beckermonds for *The Dalesman*, lamented in the late 1940s that most of these old dances were almost forgotten, which was a pity. "In another generation all trace of them will most likely have disappeared." Florence noted that the old dances have very musical names—Buttered Peas, Square Eight, Swinging Six and Huntsman's Chorus. Quadrilles bear some resemble to the Square Eight, but she thought they were of different origin. Swinging Six has been danced to the tune of *Pop Goes the Weasel* and lives up to its name, "for the whole thing goes with a swing." On the Saturday night, in the Old School at the head of Langstrothdale, the Elders of the Dale danced a Square Eight. "It was even then dying out. I well remember how astonished I was to see my parents get up and dance in this. It is, in fact, the only time I remember seeing the Square Eight danced."

In Littondale, dancing took place in a first-floor room in an outbuilding, where Tom Bolland, dubbed by Marmaduke Miller as "the last of the old Dales musicians," kept the feet of dancers clattering in a lively fashion. The man and the venue were recalled by Marmaduke in 1939. He concluded that with the advent of modern jazz bands and dance halls in most of the villages, the old type of dance which often took place in a hayloft had disappeared and, with it, the old-fashioned music that was peculier to that type of dance.

Tom Bolland played in a room which was approached by a flight of rickety stairs and had just been tidied of last year's wool clip. Piled very carefully in one corner were cow cake, crushers, bagged potatoes and sundries. Bolland would be seen jauntily perched on a milking stool, with a stout oaken 'provin' kist for a bandstand, playing on his beloved melodeon the old-time tunes such as *Yankee Doodle, Pop goes the Weasel* and *Grandfather's Clock*.

Tom wore a neckerchief, neatly tied, and had a clay pipe in his mouth. Sometimes, the pipe was the right side up, and more often it was otherwise. Old Bolland's eyes twinkled mischievously and one foot relentlessly beat out time to the music, whether it be a stately waltz or tumultuous polka. To any lad who was slow to select a partner for a dance, he would shout "Cummin lad."

In Upper Wharfedale, during the early 1980s, old dales nights were held in Grassington Town Hall at which some of the old Dales dances were revived. They included Brass Nuts and Buttered Peas. Tim Boothman gave his services freely to the Upper Wharfedale Museum Society as they tried to preserve not only the physical relics of the district but the cultural activities as well.

In constricted upstairs accommodation at Muker in Swaledale, the company included farm lads from a wide area, one of whom told me of the sometimes hazardous double crossing of the Buttertubs Pass by night. "My bike was tied up with snare wire and pieces of string. I had a few snares in my pocket in case the bike broke down. We had carbide lamps, and they gave out such a stink!" It was not the only thing which stank. Farm lads from higher up the dale rode into the village on horseback, and the horses were stabled underneath. An 'earthy' smell rose to where the dalesfolk were dancing.

This was the period when Billy Bowman's Band provided much of the music. "He had an imitation donkey (a donkey's head on a stick) and if the dancing flagged, he got astride and went round the platform, singing at the top of his voice." Other dances were held in the lower room of the Institute, with concertina and melodeons being played by such stalwarts as James Hutchinson, gamekeeper, and John Whitfield, one-time postman.

When dances were held in the Market Hall at Hawes, a piano and fiddle were available. The men had to wear gloves. "At Hawes, there was a Liberal Club and a Conservative Club, and each had its annual ball. There was a shout if any of the Conservatives went to the Liberal ball, and vice versa. In those days, folk were really clannish."

Claude Barton, agent for the Farrers at Clapham, held dancing classes in the village and, being enthusiastic about dancing and well-connected, he introduced the latest steps. One of his students, a farm lad, made a good impression at a dance in Mallerstang. The band, from Kirkby Stephen, attracted a girl who could do the latest steps but who did not expect anyone at the dance to be able to partner. The lad from Clapham obliged. Incidentally, he had travelled to Mallerstang on a motor bike. Arriving early, he went rabbiting, attended the dance, stayed overnight in the dale and returned home on the following afternoon.

At a 'village hop' in Craven, a rough wooden floor did not encourage dancing so one of the stewards scattered a packet of *Lux* all over it to make it slippery. During the first few dances, those who took part sneezed their heads off. The kitchen was so small, people went for their supper in groups of twelve. "Mother cooked a whole ham for the sandwiches. She was a good carver, making the slices very thin. There were lots of home-made cakes. By the time everyone had drunk and eaten, it was getting on for one o'clock, and the dance went on until two..."

At Settle lived Henry (Harry) Wilson, a musical blacksmith—a man who worked at the anvil during the day and, on many a night, set off with members of his family to provide music at the 'flutters' and 'hops' of Dales villages. He first played at dances when he was fourteen years old and living at Long Preston. Harry Wilson's Band sprang into action just before the 1914-18 war and Harry himself had been a player since the dawn of the century.

Apart from the Dales 'hops' and 'flutters', he also recalled fine balls, held in some of the big hostelries of Settle, when the gentlemen wore evening dress, with white bow ties and white gloves. Those were the days of programme cards, when requests for dances were jotted down and there were few 'casual' dances. Harry recalled attending a dance in the Reading Room at Stainforth when the band consisted of violin and flute and the players were accommodated on a billards table.

Kit Graham's band, which used to play at this time, took a piano with them on a flat cart. The other music-maker was a violinist. Kit charged 15s for musical accompaniment which continued until 2 a.m. The next dance Harry remembered was held in the Temperance Hotel at Hellifield. His uncle was the violinist and someone vamped on the piano. At the interval, uncle asked Harry to take a turn and play with him.

Harry was so thrilled by the experience a band was formed in his family, his sisters playing piano and violin, his father with double bass and himself playing a flute. For special occasions they had the addition of a cornet or clarinet. If two or three players were required for a dance, they would cycle to the hall, but for four and over a cab or wagonette was hired or they travelled by train. In one week, he was out and about every night except Sunday in addition to following his daily work. He had only twenty hours' sleep. One night he presented a programme of seventeen different old-time dances in one night.

In 1925, Harry played for what was literally a barn dance, held in a barn at Douk Ghyll, with a cart cover placed across the doors to subdue a frolicsome draught. The barn was unheated, of course. Harry and two companions kept on their coats and mittens. They were paid 10s each for the dance, which started at 8 p.m., had a short interval for supper, and then continued until 4 a.m., when those who stayed to the last had just enough time to get home and change before they were due to milk the cows. Harry handed the Burnley man who played the violin 2s out of the money he had personally received. The man was delighted and said: "If I hadn't come to this dance I was going to borrow 10s to go off with Burnley Football team, so I'm 22s better off." He then prepared to travel back to Burnley—on a bike!

Cycling to and from dances had its discomforts on rainy days. He was returning from Horton-in-Ribblesdale one wet morning when a gust of wind blew the cape over his head and he fell from his bike, alighting in a ditch full of water. On a snowy day, he arrived home after playing at Horton to find he had lost the music for twelve of his favourite waltzes. In the morning, he returned to Horton in the snow and was told by the caretaker of the hall that the copies were found strewn across the snowy road.

Horton and Austwick had supper dances for which 2s.6d was charged. Supper was of the knife and fork variety, with beef and ham that fell to pieces at a glance, and all kinds of cakes, trifles and jellies. "I just played until they couldn't dance," he was to recall. Occasionally that time was 6 a.m. For a dance at Austwick, the violinist turned up on horseback. When the dance ended at 4 a.m., it was snowing hard and the roads were treacherous. Harry's skill as a blacksmith came into use when he opened up the Austwick smithy and 'frost-nailed' the shoes of the horse.

He had strong views on dance music generally. He lamented the habit of singing to dance tunes. "If some of these new singers came to your door, you'd probably give them a copper to move into the next street." He denounced fifty-fifty dances, a blend of old and new, and said that modern bands were out of place playing old-time music; "they are out of tune and don't play the music as it's written. Old-time dance music should be as good to listen to as it is to dance to, and there should be an old-time combination of instruments."

Dales dances rarely began on time. A veteran dancer relates: "Part of the fun was lifting the elbow at the nearest inn." Within easy memory were days when people danced wherever there was room; where they would not become 'leg-locked'. At Muker, in Swaledale, dances took place in a room near The Farmer's Arms.

Much more robust were the farmers' dances, such as those held at Bentham. A farmer's son who cycled ten miles to a dance was on his feet virtually all the time until 2 a.m. and then he cycled home. For the Primrose League annual ball, this same youth caught the last train to Bentham, danced until 3 a.m. or 4 a.m., found shelter to play cards with friends and caught the first train home.

(Dan Binns)

Dales dancers continued to be a tough breed, undeterred by a few flakes of snow. One old couple I knew well drove home from Dent to Settle on a snowy road which had shrunk to the width of the council's plough. If it snows, then there's bound to be a few flakes at Tosside, between Ribblesdale and Bowland. It's an astonishing place, one of the dancers related. "It's out on a blooming hilltop, miles from anywhere, yet t'dances allus go off well."

An illustrious name in the story of Dales dancing is that of Beresford, a family associated in particular with the head reaches of Wharfe and Ribble. They first settled in the Dales in 1783. Peter Beresford, a native of Hartington, is known to have been manager of a smelt mill at Buckden in 1805, and members of the Beresford family farmed at Yockenthwaite in

Langstrothdale, from 1843 until 1967. Having marital connections with the Metcalfes meant they were a numerous family, and the Beresford Society has a membership of over 1,000, there being strong associations with Derbyshire and Ireland.

Musically, the tradition of playing concertina and fiddle at dances began about 120 years ago and continues to this day when Peter Beresford and his wife Mary play at Dales dances, Peter having a piano accordion and Mary operating drums. He recalls when his grandfather Beresford and great uncle Tom played violins for dancing in the Buckden area and he joined the family band, playing drums while he was still at school. Peter was a self-taught accordionist, practising in the privy at the back of the house. At the age of seventeen, he was playing with his father Jackie at Oughtershaw.

Peter and Mary have a style of playing which is distinctively Dales. Most of the dances are of the old-time variety and most of the dancers are 'getting on in years' but have retained their spriteliness on the dance floor.

It was at Tosside that I first met Harry Cockerill, of Askrigg, a somewhat legendary accordion player who imparted the

old Dales flavour to each dance. Harry "played by ear; I don't know a note o' music." His fans were generally the middle-aged and older folk who were unimpressed by flashing lights and electronic wizardry. Harry told me: "My type of dance music is just the same as it's ever been. I can't play any different." A pause. "I've played t'same tunes ever since I started—and they still dance to 'em!"

Harry perfected his technique at High Greenfield, a solitary farm "on the old packhorse road from Wharfedale to Horton." When his father moved to a farm in Bishopdale, and before Harry was married, he "lived by missen" for six years and "being one and a-half miles from the next door neighbour, I found it was ideal for practicing the accordion." His first venture in the musical world was playing for a children's party at Christmas. He went on to play at innumerable parties and enjoyed entertaining young people. From attending parties at Oughtershaw, Buckden and Stalling Busk, he 'got promoted' to Kettlewell.

Normally, Harry was a diffident, even shy man, but at dances he was assured, smiling broadly at the passing dancers, most of whom were personal friends. He told me of dances held in the Institute at Oughtershaw, which was a fairly long room, the space being restricted by the presence of a full-sized billiards table. When not being used for billiards, it was covered with boards. It was on these boards that chairs were sent for the band when dancing took place.

In the 1930s, Harry began his long association with Stalling Busk. It was the time of a Royal occasion, "when every band, even those that are not so good, gets a booking—that's where I came in!" Transport from High Greenfield to Stalling Busk was never easy. When he had a motor bike, he would fasten his accordion in its case to the machine, using cow bands.

Harry used to chuckle at the remembrance of an old Army hut in Coverdale. The hut had a sloping floor, with the stove at the lowest point. Two chaps, who were merry, did not make sufficient allowance for the gradient. "I remember how capped (surprised) they were as they staggered towards yon stove." Tradition counts for a lot in the upper dales. At Stalling Busk, dances were held in the old Schoolroom. Gradually they began to tail away, but Harry's enthusiasm was undimmed. I remember talking to a dancer who said "we have a round of dominoes, then supper, and then t'dance. There were about ten couples t'other neet. We've getten down to not so many."

Traditionally, dancing was of secondary importance to arm-raising exercises at the local inn. In the days of hard drinking, many a dance did not start until midnight. "The dancers nivver knocked off before two, and many a time it got to three. I used to fodder cows at t'outbarns on my way home. Sometimes, when I got home, I didn't know if t'moon was going to bed or t'sun was getting up!"

HIGH DALE COUNTRY
Raking hay near
Thwaite, in Swaledale.

Above: A dalesman and his dogs. Thomas Joy, shepherd on Grassington Moor.

Below: Swaledale sheep in stained glass, Hubberholme Church.

Cecil Slingsby, mountaineer
and friend of Edvund Grieg.

Leta Douglas, collector
of folk dances.

Below: Handel Parker (right), who composed
the hymn tune "Deep Harmony".

GUNNERSIDE. L. M.

Composed by JAS REYNOLDSON, Burnley
Inscribed to the Memory of my son JOHN,
who was killed in the Great War.

O Love of God, how strong and true;
E - ter - nal and yet ev - er new:
Un - com - pre - hend - ed and un - bought, Be - yond all know - ledge and all thought.

Proceeds devoted to the National Children's Home and Orphanage.

Jas Reynoldson composed the hymn tunes "Muker" and "Gunnerside" to the memory of his son, killed in the 1914-18 war.

Harry Cockerill, one of the last of the old time accordionists.

A Wulstan Atkins, godson of Edward Elgar, on a brief visit to Crackpot Farm, Swaledale. Elgar had several holidays in North Ribblesdale.

TWO "TERRIBLE" KNITTERS

Elizabeth Middleton and Doris Hartley demonstrate local hand-knitting and sing some old songs.

The word "terrible" in the Dales context means "great".

Below: A knitting stick, as used in Dentdale.

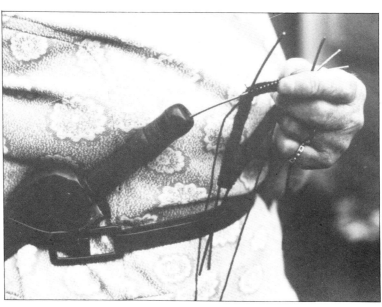

NOTABLE COMPOSERS

Top, left—Edward Elgar.

Top, right—Frederick Delius.

Left—Roger Quilter, who visited the Settle area several times just after the 1939-45 war.

SINGING ABOUT THE SETTLE-CARLISLE

Dave Goulder (right) and the late Mike Donald, writers of the best songs about the famous railway.

Pace Eggers and Horse Dealers

D R CHARLES William Buck, of Giggleswick, now best-known through his long friendship with the composer Elgar, which began when the two young men met in Worcester in 1882, was keen on collecting folk music. It is a tribute to Elgar's generosity of spirit that when Buck raised this topic, he listened with patience. And when Buck requested that his friend might harmonise or orchestrate a melody he had collected in the locality he promptly obliged.

A case in point was the Pace Eggers' play. Basically drama, it was sometimes referred to as *The Play of St George* and related to a folk-ritual going back to pagan times and dealing with the triumph of summer over winter. Arthur Raistrick, the Dales historian, observed that a superficial observer might think of the *Pace Egg Play*, also known as *The Mummers' Play*, as merely slapstick comedy. "Rather should one stand in awe and respect before a fragment of man's earliest dramatisation of his religious beliefs." This was, indeed, "a fossil from the mind of earliest man."

Nationally, at least thirty versions of this ancient drama are known. The Pace Eggers were active at Easter and the Mummers went forth on Old Year's Night. The pagan element had eventually been Christianised by the substitution of St George killing the Dragon, thus liberating the Princess Sabra. When there was a surge of popular feeling about the Crusades, St George had turned his sword on a Turkish knight.

Dr Buck, sad that by the late 19th century the Play had become "an interesting ruin, patched up in various ways by many hands," became quite obsessive in his plan to produce it in the Craven district, where research indicated that the characters now included two naval heroes, Nelson and Collingwood, the full cast being Fool, Slasher, St George, Nelson, Collingwood, Jack Tar, Miser and Tosspot. Music was provided by fiddle or medodeon or both.

The Vicar of Giggleswick assisted Buck, at much cost of time and postage, to contact country folk in many parts of Britain, and thus to gather and amalgamate fragments of the Pace Eggers' play. Any Dales element was thus diluted. The *Ancient Mystery Play of St George* was presented, with considerable advance publicity, in the Victoria Hall at Settle, on Easter Tuesday, 1894. A play which normally was enacted out of doors, often in bitter weather, now had a weatherproof setting, the whole programme having the support of a thirty-four piece orchestra. Naturally, the conductor was Buck himself. He had persuaded his great friend Elgar to write 'a musical setting', but if Elgar brought himself to do such a thing the score has been lost.

The *Ancient Mystery Play* having been introduced by the Rev A Crofton, it was performed at a lively pace. The Fool set the style:

> We're two or three jolly boys, all of one mind,
> We're come a pace-egging and hope you'll prove kind,
> For we're come to repeat you our ancientry rhyme,
> And we hope you'll remember it's pace-egging time.

Each verse was followed by a chorus:

> Laddi fol de day, Laddi fol,
> Laddie fol de laral-i-day.

Afterwards, in the varied programme prepared for the musical event in the Victoria Hall, came the 'old English song', *The Painful Pleugh*, rendered by Mr Handby. Buck had himself been known to sing it. He usually remarked in advance that the word 'painful' was used in its original meaning of painstaking. The opening lines of the song were indeed painful:

Come all you jolly pleughmen
　　Of course stout and bold
That labours all the winter
　　Thro' stormy winds and cold,
To clothe your fields with plenty,
　　Your harvest to renew,
We crown them with contentment
　　That holds the painful pleugh.

Buck readily admitted that the 'traditional songs' he collected were primitive. "They have a good deal of 'fol de rol' in the chorus like most folk tunes," he wrote, while insisting that they must not be forgotten. The Pace Egging piece was his best effort. He was proud of his research, asserting it was a great pity that many songs should be lost to future generations "for the modern comic song with its vulgarities seems to have ousted the old friends...We should do all we can to preserve these quaint songs and amusements which pleased our fore-elders and which few now living can remember."

In 1947, the Malham and Rathmell drama classes performed the Pace Egg Play at the last-named village and later round the cross in Settle Market Place and in Malham, where Reg Clarke was persuaded to stroll on ahead of the band of 23 players rendering the ancient air *Greensleeves* on his violin. The version of the play used had been unearthed by Arthur Raistrick. Production was by Mrs William Mason, of Airton, who also wrote extra dialogue, including a prologue and 'hecklings' to be shouted by people in the crowd. Mrs Mason provided crowns made from linoleum and many other 'props'.

The Victorian doctor, Charles William Buck, put almost as much effort into his music as he did into doctoring. Nearly all his spare time was spent with with music-related interests. He looked for the rough old songs such as were sung at rent dinners, at weddings and Christmas festivities. "They are often associated with hunting or horse-dealing, as befits the

Yorkshire Tyke,'' he wrote. One old ballad, known as *Clapham Town End* or The Yorkshire Horse Dealers, haunted him. It was a typical Victorian ballad, with an amusing twist in the last verse.

The ballad was named after the greystone village of Clapham, which lies almost in the shadow of Ingleborough, and where the New Inn was already fairly old. Buck jotted down the melody from a rendering of one Tommy Kerr. He also collected the words. In 1890, his friend Elgar consented, as an act of friendship, to harmonise the melody. Elgar took immediate action—and posted it back to Giggleswick by return. It was as though he was anxious to see the last of it!

Not only does *Clapham Town End* preserve a traditional tale in verse; it also enshrines some of the old Craven dialect. The story, dating to the early part of last century, concerned a Yorkshire tyke known as Tommy Towers, who gloried in his success as a horse-dealer.

Tommy owned a horse that was just skin-and-bone. It was time to dispose of it before it died. A neighbour, Abraham Muggins, who was also crafty in horse-dealing, wanted to sell a horse without letting the other man know it had died. Abraham decided he would swap this horse for what he believed to be Tommy's live horse. The two men met to discuss the matter. After the usual haggling, the swap was arranged, whereupon Abraham (incidentally, a sobriquet for a former Clapham innkeeper) announced that the horse was dead. Tommy then mentioned the death of his horse, which had been skinned. Tommy had the better bargain, being richer—by a hide and four horseshoes!

> Bane to Claapham town-gate lived an oud Yorkshire tyke,
> Who i' dealing i' horselflesh hed ne'er met his like;
> 'Twor his pride that i' aw the hard bargains he'd hit,
> He'd bit a girt monny, but nivver bin bit.
>
> Chorus: With my dum a dum dary, &c.

Although stated to be "Harmonised by Sir Ed. Elgar", neither the score nor the words are in Elgar's handwriting. He wrote: "The Melody of C.W.B." It was signed "Edward Elgar", the date being September 15, 1885.

This oud Tommy Towers (bi that naam he wor knaan),
Hed an ould crikon tit that wor sheer skin an' baan;
Ta hev killed him for t'curs wad hev bin quite as well
But t'wor Tommy's opinion he'd dee of hissel!

Chorus

Well! yan Abraham Muggings, a neighbouring cheat,
Thowt ta diddle oud Tommy wa'd be a rare treat;
He'd a horse, too, 'twor war than ould Tommy's ye see,
Fort-neet afore that he'd thowt proper ta dee!

Chorus

Thinks Abey, t'oud codger 'il nivver smoak t'trick,
I'll swop wi' him my poor deead horse for his wick,
An' if Tommy I nobbut can happen ta trap,
'Twill be a fine feather i' Aberram's cap!

Chorus

Soa to Tommy he goas, an' t'question he pops:
'Between thy horse and mine, prithee, Tommy, what swops?
What wilt gi' me ta boot? for mine's better horse still!'
'Nout,' says Tommy, 'I'll swop ivven hands, an' ye will.'

Chorus

Abey preaached a lang time about summat ta boot,
Insistin' that his war t'liveliest brute;
But Tommy stuck fast where he first had begun
Till Abey wagged hands, and sed, 'Done, Tommy, done!'

Chorus

'Eh Tommy,' my lad, 'I'ze sorry for thee,
I thowt thou'd a getten mair white i' thy ee;
Good luck wi' thy bargin, for my horse is deead.'
'Why, hang it,' says Tommy, 'soa's mine, an its fleead!'

Chorus

Soa Tommy got t'better of t'bargain, a vast,
An' cam' off wi' a Yorkshireman's triumph at last;
For twixt two deead horses there's not mitch to choose,
Yet Tommy war richer by t'hide an'fower shooes.

Chorus

Buck's task with *Clapham Town End* was relatively simple—it was to memorise the little tune and a chorus and write them down. Elgar harmonised "in strict accord with the spirit of the age." I like the tune and Elgar's treatment of it. The words of this song, the melody and Elgar's contribution were among the signed scores given to me on a summer's day in 1989 by the lady who had inherited them from Monica, the daughter of Dr Buck.

The doctor's folk song collection included *Old Adam*, which (he asserted) was sung at Giggleswick weddings by Betty Stockdale until about 1850. Betty first recited a toast:

> Here's a health to the bride,
> Likewise the bridegroom.
> Here's also a health to all in this room.
> I wish them health, I wish them wealth,
> I wish them gold in store;
> I wish them Heaven when they die,
> What can I wish them more?

Buck's love of music led him to encourage village children to take up the violin. A visitor to the National School at Giggleswick might see a group of children busily 'scraping away' in a classroom, with the doctor offering every encouragement. Buck came into his own when he conducted the orchestra at the annual show of the Settle Amateur Operatic Society, held in the Victoria Hall.

Arthur Wood's Maypole

A Maypole Dance representing Barwick Green in Arthur Wood's *My Native Heath* is the lively introduction to the radio series *The Archers*. Two versions are currently used in the broadcast of the programmes, one version from Monday to Friday inclusive having been recorded specifically for the use of the radio production. The version used at the beginning of the Sunday omnibus was recorded by *The Yetties* on an album called *Up Market* released on the Decca label (SKL/5282), an album which is not currently available. The tune has been played a myriad times and yet comes up fresh every time.

The Dalesfolk offset the melancholy of the long, long winters by attending dances. Some of the old steps are still to be seen amid the more flamboyant olde-time and modern dances, the last-named giving the impression by their intricacy that they have been devised by computer. Now there's line-dancing. It is no longer necessary to have a partner. In summer, there was maypole dancing at such places at Kettlewell and Long Preston, where maypoles might still be seen.

The lively music composed by Arthur Wood, and used so effectively by *The Archers*, is a Maypole Dance inspired by Barwick, being part of a suite which is completed by Knaresborough (hirings), Ilkley Tarn and Bolton Abbey. Hardly anyone knows the other delightful pieces in the suite. Nor is much known generally about the composer of what, by its constant repetition in a much-loved radio story, is arguably among the Top Ten in popularity.

Arthur Wood was born in 1875, his natal town being Heckmondwike. He grew up amid the muck and mills and pits. His family were tailors during the week and on Sunday drew spiritual strength from attending Chapel, more precisely T'Upper Chapel. Young Arthur played his flute for chapel concerts.

73

Lyn Arnold, his daughter, recalled for *Dalesman* readers that as a small girl she was present at the first performance of his folk-dance suit, *Three Yorkshire Dale Dances*. Father, a lovable, unpretentious man, sat at the family's upright piano and added vocally to the piano line his orchestral effects. Lyn Arnold's uncle stopped him half way through, observing: "Yes, a real piece of work, I think—but dear boy, don't sing!"

The Wood family moved to Harrogate in 1882. Arthur's father continued his tailoring by day but really came alive in the evening when he played second viola in the theatre orchestra. He boasted that he had never missed a performance in four decades. Arthur began his musical career as a small boy chorister at St Peter's Church. In later years, he told of how he began as an instrumentalist when his father, dissatisfied with his progress on the violin, bought him a one-key piccolo, which cost half a crown, and threw it to him across the table at breakfast one day with the words: "Practice that."

Soon, Arthur had turned to the piccolo's elder brother, the flute. He became an accomplished flautist and also concentrated on the keyboard. At the age of 14, he was appointed organist of St Paul's Presbyterian Church, Harrogate. The family's early years in Harrogate had been attended by poverty, and yet the sparse conditions were forgotten whenever there was time for music-making. The Wood family was large enough to have its own choral group and gave parlour performances of oratorios, including *Elijah* and *The Messiah!*

Arthur, an accomplished flautist, was engaged to play in the orchestra of the Town Hall Theatre and, aged sixteen, he became deputy conductor, solo flautist and pianist of the Spa Orchestra in the Royal Spa Rooms. His next next move was to Bournmouth, where he played under Sir Dan Godfrey, thence to London in 1903, as musical director of Terry's Theatre. At the age of twenty-eight, he was the youngest musical director in London.

It was the start of a thirty year association as conductor with a number of theatres, yet Arthur Wood never forgot his northern roots and family outings to the Yorkshire Dales, especially Upper Wharfedale. When he re-visited Harrogate professionally, he was usually asked to conduct his own works, especially *My Native Heath* and what became 'the Archers' tune'. He kept his Yorkshire feet firmly on the ground. When Lyn, his daughter, returned home from a party and reported she had tasted caviare, father remarked: "Acquire the taste for caviare by all means—provided you don't lose your taste for kippers."

The day before he died at his London home, in January, 1953, Arthur Wood—poor in eyesight, weak in health—insisted with Yorkshire stubbornness/courage on bringing in the coals for the fire.

Kendal Ghyll.

A folk dance collected by Leta Douglas.

Leta Douglas:
Folk Dancer Extraordinary

F OR many, the 1930s were lean years, a period of industrial depression. Many working class folk in the North Country, looking for cheap ways of escaping from the murk and misery of the mill towns, re-discovered the Dales countryside. Some were returning to areas such as Swaledale from which, a generation or two before, their forebears had emigrated following the closure of the lead mines.

The day-tripper from town walked in everyday clothes, with hob-nailed boots on his feet and a packet of sandwiches in his rucksack. Those who went by bike might cover sixty and more miles in the day. Some cyclists, returning home via Malham, bought a slice of Mrs Brown's fruit-cake to give them sustenance for the last few punishing miles home.

Vaughan Williams and his friends had already explored the countryside, collecting old folk tunes and re-presenting them in orchestral form. So the new outdoor movement had its theme tunes, notably *Greensleeves*. Cecil Sharp had become nationally renowned for his researches into traditional folk dances. In the Dales, Leta Douglas, of Giggleswick, inculcated an interest in folk dancing, raising one, then two teams of dancers in the Settle area. Each year, when the weather might be expected to be kind, they toured the Craven Dales, dancing on village greens.

If that had been all, the teams and Leta herself would have been forgotten, but she had also persuaded old-timers in the Dales villages to tell her about the dances they had enjoyed and to hum the old tunes. Leta's findings were published in two collections. The first, *Six Dances of the Yorkshire Dales*, appeared in November, 1931, when she was living in Giggleswick. This collection ran to thirteen editions. Copies were sent to the United States, to Singapore, New Zealand and South Africa. The second collection, *Three More Dances of the Yorkshire Dales*, together with The Boosbeck Traditional Long Sword Dance, had by 1934 attained its seventh edition.

Leta's work in the elementary schools of the district was centred on Settle and enabled her to become friendly with the Dalesfolk who were willing to help in the revival of the old dances. The first dance she collected was Meeting Six. It was demonstrated to her during a morning playtime in one of the schools and was still being danced quite often at Kettlewell. Leta now planned a Whit-week tour of Wharfedale, which was maintained for nine successive years.

Fred Falshaw, of Buckden, taught the dancers Meeting Six, and also recalled Buttered Peas and Kendal Ghyll. On the same glorious day, George Turnbull, who farmed at Oughtershaw, taught the visitors Turn off Six. When the team was shown the steps of Huntsman's Chorus by Mrs R Metcalfe of Grassington, they could hardly imagine its success. Huntsman's Chorus became the most popular of all those which Leta collected. She received a letter from an American dance club stating that Huntsman's Chorus was always on the programme.

In her second book, Leta thanked two Wharfedale stalwarts, the aforementioned Fred Falshaw and Sam Stables of Grassington. Help had also been forthcoming from Fred Thorugood of Gisburn and Fred Towler of Selside. The sword dance tune was recalled by George Tremain, of North Skelton in Cleveland.

Joe Parker of Stackhouse and Fred Harrison of Paythorne provided music to keep the feet tapping at a special gathering which took place in Rathmell Reading Room in 1929. Robert Brook, of School House, at Leta's request, had called together the folk who knew the old dances. Leta recorded that ''nothing seemed to tire the old people. We finished up with a polka. Tom Robinson quite danced his partner off her feet. Mrs Frankland of Little Bank, Tom Robinson and Phineas Harrison showed us some Yorkshire step-dancing..." The Yorkshire Square Eight was collected at about this time. (Tom Harrison eventually went off his legs and was transported in a bath-chair. On visits to Settle, he often stopped for a chat with Leta Douglas and her friends).

Leta's enthusiasm for folk-dancing knew no bounds. She took some visiting dancers to the Settle smithy so they might enjoy "the acrid smell, the blazing fire, the roar of the bellows, the ring of the anvil, the patient horse which lifts its hoof with such confidence..." When the horse had been shod by Reg Hodgson, she mentioned that he had made the swords the students would be using in the traditional Yorkshire Longsword Dance they were on their way to learn.

Competing at York, Settle entered two teams and won first prizes in their sections. The adjudicator paid tribute to the dancing of both teams and also recognised the worth of the Settle accompanist, James Allen, who played the melodeon. He was complimented on his rhythmic playing. James's love of music sprang from that of his mother, who was a native of Hawes. He was familiar with the Dales way of playing. He loved the old tunes and had no time for modern music.

When he first joined the dancers, all that was necessary was for someone to hum or sing an air and James Allen would strike up. For many years, he was a well-known figure leading the dancers in a Processional Dance through the Wharfedale villages. Leta was to write: "When on the last tour he was too ill to go, at every village people asked where he was and the dancers missed his music."

At a later period, Eddie Percy of Giggleswick was sometimes in attendance when Miss Douglas took her dancers to Wharfedale. Eddie mounted a 12-volt gramophone player on his vehicle. Miss Douglas herself caused a minor sensation in North Craven as she motored around the schools. She was the proud owner of a belt-driven Trojan.

Huntsman's Chorus.

Ironically, she died when, having got out of her own car on a winter day to help the owner of a car which had broken down, she suffered a broken pelvis when another car ran into it from behind. She was taken to hospital and died here.

The mortal remains of Leta Douglas were interred in Giggleswick churchyard on January 5, 1951.

J Sutcliffe Smith: A Musical Pilgrim

Between the Wars, Dr J Sutcliffe Smith of Harrogate toured Yorkshire, looking for evidence of music and musicians. He recorded what he found in articles and two books—*A Musical Pilgrimage in Yorkshire* and *The Music of the Yorkshire Dales*. The second book consisted of letters to a friend, Donald, a native of Skipton whom he had met at the Leeds Musical Festival of 1928. *Musical Pilgrimage* had just been published. The letters, sent to Donald, who was living in Scotland, were later gathered together for publication.

Smith merits a section to himself. His books might have been more sharply edited. He tended to make mountains out of mole-hills, and yet to remove the trivial and irrelevant paragraphs would rob the work of that delicate factor called 'charm'. Smith had clear memories of the start of his musical pilgrimage. "A glance at a map of Yorkshire brings me a host of reminders. Near the centre, I see Harrogate, where, on a certain bright Sunday, the thought of writing about Yorkshire music came into my mind. This was on the Stray, and I can picture the very spot. There as I sat and pondered what such a task would entail, I saw before me much travelling, many interviews and a good deal of research. But I was enthusiastic and determined to go through with it."

Having published *The Musical Pilgrimage of Yorkshire*, he felt there was much more to be discovered. "Those fascinating places known as the Yorkshire dales had, I found, a musical story quite their own—a story that told how song was very much alive there hundreds of years ago and how many generations back, in the lone farmstead of Nidderdale and elsewhere, there was concerted music wherein pipes and fiddles played their part. In my *Music of the Yorkshire Dales*, I made it my endeavour to show what an important part the dalesfolk took in building up those great traditions..."

He recounted some of his adventures for readers of *The Yorkshire Dalesman*, as the popular magazine *The Dalesman* was then known. "At the head of Swaledale is the old Cathole Inn where I stayed more than once, and nearby is the highway where I found a roadmender who played the cornet and composed hymn tunes. In a hayfield higher up the dale, I rubbed shoulders with a farmer who sang a war song of his own which he told me had come into mind during one of the nights of the Great War."

In Nidderdale, he sat and chatted with a musical miller who knew how to train a choir and who told him how one of his ancestors had formed a band. "At his tea table I was always a welcome guest; and in this same dale I had the good fortune to meet an old man who had made quite a study of local musical history and was proud to have known Ben Jackson, who lived at Birstwith, and later became organist at The Alexandra Palace, London."

Smith's world of live music was under threat from the wireless. He agreed with Donald, his Scottish friend, that the tone was poor and thin and the sound often, as it were, "throttled and colourless...and the total result a mere travesty of the true vocal quality or orchestral effect". Also the Talkies (cinema) was another failure from an art point of view, with a tone that was "nasal, blatant and ugly, with no redeeming feature beyond the wonder of it all." Later, he heard something better—the tone more modulated, and the singing more sympathetic, "from which I concluded that the Talkies may have a great future before them."

We do not know a great deal about the man called Donald. He was recalled by his friend Smith in relation to "those hair-brained days when we shivered in a hut near the Solway in order to get a particular view." They had a 'sousing' near Loch Earn Head when they dallied overlong among the bonnie braes of Aberfeldy.

It was at Leeds, following the publication of A Musical Pilgrimage, that Donald had suggested further research might be undertaken. His friend must go "not only into the highways, but also the byways of Yorkshire, and try to discover the foundations of the county's great musical position in this England of ours; in other words that I should scour its moors and dales and prove, if possible, that Yorkshire music is really Yorkshire; and has not been so dependent on imported talent as some are inclined to suppose."

First, Donald's idea simmered, next it became hot, and now it has reached boiling point, he wrote in the introductory letter to The Music of the Yorkshire Dales. "In short, I am determined to make those excursions, and find out what our more isolated dwellers are doing, or have done, towards Yorkshire's grand sum total of music." He also looked forward to enjoying the grand scenery and to having "a touch of adventure," which included bus-riding and walking.

Brisk sales for his book were ensured when he inscribed it, "by permission," to Sir William Ingilby, Bart., and The Honourable Lady Ingilby, of Ripley Castle, Nidderdale, "both active Workers in the Cause of Music." Swaledale was his first choice. He started far down, at Catterick, but had soon progressed to the upper dale, where he hoped to meet Richard Alderson, nicknamed Neddy Dick, a character I mentioned in the introduction, whom Smith romantically termed "the musician of the mountains." Neddy, he had heard, "made a musical scale with stones taken from the bed of the Swale." Smith asked a fellow passenger in the Swaledale bus as to whether Neddy was still living at Keld, to be told: "He is dead; he died quite a while back."

At a local inn, the Cathole, Mrs Hutchinson remarked that

Neddy died some two years before. He left her his harmonium, which was in one of the front rooms, and his bells he had suspended from it, with which he had produced "remarkable and often surprising effects," had gone to a relative in Skipton. Mrs Hutchinson pointed to a grandfather clock standing on the staircase and said that Neddy had often asked her for the bell belonging to it so that he might complete his set. The stones were, as related, in the ruins of an outhouse.

Neddy Dick was described by a local man who knew him as "a queer un. He wer brought up to farming; but his mind was always running on music. He neglected himself badly; and though he had money he didn't know how to use it. Lots o' fowk came to hear him play on t'stones he had fished up out o' t'beck." Smith met another man who had known Neddy. This time it was "a cultural musician," who had stayed in Keld while Neddy was still alive.

He was impressed by Neddy's musical ability. "On his stones, which had been selected with the utmost care, and tuned by chipping, he rapped out many melodies with facility. His harmonium, with bells attached to a framework, made a happy combination. With one hand he played an accompaniment on the instrument; while with the other he chimed the melody on the bells."

With this miniature orchestra, he produced delightful effects and charmed the many visitors who came to his cottage during the summer months. "When I sang to him the tune to 'Leeds Owd Kirk', he became quite excited and quickly appropriated it with his own special treatment." The cultural musician regarded Neddy as "one who possessed genius—musical and inventive."

Smith summed up what he had heard of the man with these words: "So strong in him was music, that to follow it he gave up his farm and even neglected his personal comfort. With full advantages, what might not such a one have done? In a humble manner he resembled Beethoven: he was careless about money, he sadly neglected his well-being, and by many he was doubtless regarded not only as an eccentric but as something approaching a madman.''

Donald responded to the first letter by buying a map of Yorkshire and, with the help of a microscope, had fixed the position of Keld. His friend Smith attended a concert at Muker, where the music hall type of entertainment was favoured. ''The singers all had pleasant voices, and what especially struck me was the applause given to the best pieces.'' At Hardraw, in Wensleydale, he visited ''the battle-field of bands''—namely, the steep-sided little valley below the scaur which, he described as ''a concert room through which a river constantly makes its way . . . a room where tonal effects are kept well balanced.''

In his wanderings through Wensleydale, he chatted with local people about the choral societies which had proliferated. Miss Burrill sent him two of her folk song discoveries—*Pace Egging Song* (heard at the New Year) and *Ensilver* (sung when drinking the health of the bride at a public house). At the village of Wensley he heard of the achievements of the Hon Lucien Orde-Powlett (1855-1905) who was a performer, conductor and supporter of musical interests. He was organist at Leyburn and Wensley churches. He instigated the Wensleydale and Swaledale Tournaments of Song, which did much to stimulate rural music in Yorkshire.

At Leyburn, he heard of Willie Wrigley, a fastidious fiddler, who when he required a new string spurned those available locally and walked to and from a shop in Leeds. And at Masham he was proud of his re-discovery of William Jackson, born here in 1816. Among his many musical compositions was an oratorio, *The Deliverance of Israel from Babylon,* the last chorus of which he composed on his twenty-ninth birthday.

The oratorio had its first performance in the Music Hall at Leeds, in 1847, and a local critic was impressed by the fact it had been conceived and completed ''without the advantage of a single trial, even of the vocal score alone, much less of those rich orchestral effects which Mr Jackson himself (equally with the audience) heard for the first time on Tuesday last." Jackson wrote a second oratorio, *Isaiah*, which was published in 1851. The composer took up residence in Bradford and was appointed conductor of the Festival Choral Society at its foundation. He was invited to take his choir to Buckingham Palace to sing before Queen Victoria.

Smith regarded Nidderdale as a valley "for story and romance...perhaps unequalled by any other part of Yorkshire." A local lady observed: "We are the most musical of the dales." Also the most versatile, with sword dancers touring the Dacre area and dancing to musical accompaniment provided by a melodeon. Nidderdale had even boasted a band composed of men with jew's harps. Smith found preserved in the collection of Ernest Abbott at Dacre a Broadwood harpsichord which was a century and a-half old; a trombone that had belonged to the Fewston Band, "an old-fashioned harp and a superannuated clarinet."

Our Musical Pilgrim visited Middlesmoor, at the dalehead, and wrote to his friend Donald about the Eglins who for about three centuries had lived at Hazel Close. They had all been musical, being the "the mainstay of the string and wind band in Middlesmoor church". They practised their instruments—violin, 'cello, oboe and clarinet—in their home; and some of the family were singers."

Tom Bradley, of Lofthouse, told him about the brass band in which he played the cornet. The band dated back to a meeting called in the schoolroom. Jim Calvert was appointed secretary and soon the instruments had been purchased. "The whole population turned out to see them brought from the train; and soon I had my hands full in teaching the recruits to play." In six months, the men were playing hymns. Not long afterwards, they gave a concert of sacred selections at Pateley Bridge. They came third in a band contest held at Muker.

At Greenhow, the lead-miners were good singers and instrumentalists. "At the little chapel, the Messiah was given with instrumental accompaniment."

A Daleswoman (Fred Lawson).

A Century of Banding

W HEN the centenary of the Settle-Carlisle Railway was being celebrated in 1976, an old-time concert was organised in the aptly-named Victoria Hall at Settle. The Giggleswick and Settle brass band was given the honour of opening the concert. We all expected a lively tune. The bandmaster referred briefly to the recent death of one of the members and, in his honour, the band played *Deep Harmony*, a hymn tune composed in the Bronte Country. For band and audience alike, it was a solemn and intensely moving experience.

Arthur Percival, born and bred in Wensleydale, was fond of recalling when he first heard 'sounding brass' in his native valley. Arthur, who was to serve nobly in the Hallë Orchestra, had "literally tingled with the sheer thrill and excitement of it" as he listened to the strains of a brass band sustained by largely self-taught dalesmen.

This contrasted with the reaction of two farmers who had just attended a Hardraw Scar band contest. Arthur Percival, then nobbut a lad, overheard one say: "Ow doesta think they played, John?" John puffed at his pipe for a long time, then said: "Verra weel. I think they played verra weel. I reckon yon lot's middlin musical. Aye...very musical." And once again he lapsed into a silence from which he would not be easily roused.

One of the most significant strands of our Dales musical heritage is the brass band. Old photographs show that wherever a dozen dalesmen gathered together—they would form a band. In the inter-war years, joining the crowds in Skipton High Street, I would listen to the local band playing a medley of favourite hymn tunes, among them *Deep Harmony*—the bandsman's special hymn.

Bandsmen seem indifferent to climatic variations. The Lofthouse and Middlesmoor band, playing at the sheep show on Tan Hill in May are not to know, at that time of year, whether the Weather Clerk will offer sunshine or sleet. The music will usually be plucked by the wind, to be spread far and wide across the moors. This band plays in the sometimes wet and windy setting of the car park near Scar House reservoir at the annual re-union of those having links with the temporary village during the construction period. The sixtieth anniversary was celebrated in 1997.

Hawes Silver Band has for years mustered by Semerwater for an annual service conducted by the vicar, who, in a scene reminiscent of Galilee, occupies a boat a little way from the shore where band and congregation have mustered. Semerwater has been a setting for outdoor services for many years. The late Dick Chapman told me that when he was a boy he and his brother swam naked across Semerwater and were unable to land near the Carlow Stone, a large ice-borne rock, because a religious service was in progress. The lads had to stand neck deep in water until they had recuperated. They then swam back to where they had left their clothes.

History books reveal that musicians from Gunnerside had accompanied the copyholders when they marched over Oxnop Gill Head on their way to vote at the polling booth in Askrigg at the first Reform Bill election in 1832. Gunnerside Band visited Reeth at feast times and, wrote Dr Margaret Batty in one of her fascinating booklets about life in Swaledale, Redmire Band came over to Tom Guy's at Grinton at Christmas. "There was a Reeth boys' Drum and Fife band, Fremington Band and Arkendale Band."

The sound of brass has a special quality when it emanates from the bandstand in the deep gorge at Hardraw, the setting for many band contests since Victorian times. In an open dale situation, as at one of the local shows, sounding brass seems to improve in quality with distance and has a haunting quality when the listener is on the nearest fellside. Muker Show would be emotionally flat if it was not for the celebrated local band, which assembles outside the inn, plays a rousing medley and is then led to the showfield by its conductor, Duncan Bythell, accompanied by the show officials. Muker band celebrated its centenary by playing a lively programme of favourite music on the actual summit of Great Shunner Fell, on 22nd June, 1997.

In the second half of the nineteenth and the first half of the twentieth centuries, the sound of brass instruments was heard throughout the Dales. For a glorious century, give or take a few years, every village had its own group of instrumentalists, who could be relied upon to march and play on special occasions. The formation of the band and its subsequent engagements were usually recorded in the parish magazine.

When in 1952 I called to see David Harker, a founder of Muker Band, he showed me a collection of magazines of special musical interest. At Muker in February, 1897, the vicar (Rev James Cooke) recorded that ''we are going to have a New Brass Band for Muker Parish, in memory of and in honour of the Queen's long reign of sixty years. I believe the amount given and promised up to the time of my writing is £20 or more. We trust a Band may prove to be useful in many ways, both to our young men and to the Parishioners generally.''

The early progress of the band might be followed in serial form. In March, the vicar wrote in fulsome style: ''We are glad to be able to state that the amount given and promised towards Muker Brass Band is now £35. The Band will cost £45, and there will be other expenses in connection with it. Therefore, we shall be grateful if any old lover of Muker, or Swaledale, living either in Lancashire or America, or anyone else, will send us their ready help.'' In April, ''the instruments for Muker Brass Band have arrived and a Band Room has been obtained in the village, where the Bandsmen now practice several nights in the week with a right down good will.''

The vicar was delighted to hear them play *God Save the Queen* and another lively tune ''quite well'' on the second night only of their practices. ''The Committee will be glad to receive further subscriptions.'' The Band first appeared in public in May: ''Muker Brass Band held their first open air practice in the Market Place, in the centre of the village, on Saturday evening, May 8th, and delighted the inhabitants with their excellent music for about an hour. £40 has already been paid for the instruments and the Committee anxiously await the coming in of further subscriptions.''

David Harker, whose mind was filled with the lore of Muker Silver Band, mentioned that in the early days the Band rehearsed by candlelight, and one of the hazards was being splattered by dripping tallow. At Christmas, Muker Band toured the dale, also Coverdale, Wensleydale and occasionally Richmond. So the bandsmen had also to be experienced walkers. ''One night we left Carperby at eleven o' clock and had to walk home over the tops. We went to dalehead farms and always got plenty to eat.''

For thirty-six years, Muker Band had never missed the Foresters' Club Walk at Carlton in Coverdale. ''When we went to Carlton, we set off from Muker at 4 a.m. and usually got back at 4 a.m. the next day. We travelled by horse and trap over the tops by Askrigg.'' Muker Band *still* plays at the Carlton in Coverdale Club Walk, which is held every other year. It is a remarkable event and probably the last of its kind in the Dales, with the Club members still parading in full regalia. In 1997, the Band was observing the 90th anniversary of their first appearance. The event has been missed only once—in 1951 when the band was almost defunct. David Harker was hoping that in Coronation year some local enthusiasts would at least 'raise a squeak'.

W S Raw, who said he was the bandmaster ''if we're doin' owt'', recalled joyful days when bands were associated with Keld, Muker, Gunnerside, Low Row and Reeth. Now he was wondering whether there'd be enough enthusiasts at Muker to "mak a do for t'Coronation." The revival of the Band after 1952 was very much the work of Mr Raw but it depended on the recruitment of a new generation of young men. Ken Guy and his cousins, the brothers Norman, Maurice and Ron Guy, are still the stalwarts of the Band after over forty years.

Says the conductor, Duncan Bythell: "It's remarkable that there are players in the Band today, such as David Harker and George Alderson, who actually played alongside some of the veterans of the original band of 1897." The Muker Band, under the baton of Duncan, is thriving. He was appointed conductor in 1985 and lives at Gunnerside, a mile or two down the dale from Muker.

The enthusiastic members of Muker Silver band gather for practise on two evenings each week in the basement of the Institute. They do not own their bandroom. They do not spend money travelling to contests—apart from that prime Dales event, the Hardraw Band Contest. At the latest count there were 32 playing members, fourteen of whom are members of the Guy family. Ken Guy is the longest serving member. His cousin Norman serves as Bandmaster. All play for the fun of the thing. Since 1965, they have been uniform-ed, but before that they turned up on special occasions in what is known in the Dales as 'best setting-off clothes'.

Duncan, in his booklet *Banding in the Dales*, "a centenary history of Muker Silver Band," used his historian's skill in ferreting out and assembling details not just of Muker but of other Dales bands and setting their history in the context of the brass band movement. The "self-appointed guardians of 'high culture'," had little time for "the noisy, enthusiastic ef-forts of self-taught and usually working class brass players." Such music was simply not Art!

The earliest newspaper references to band activities found by Duncan record their appearances in the annual 'walks' of friendly societies—the local lodges of the Foresters, the Shepherds or the Oddfellows—which proliferated in the

dales villages in the 1830s and 1840s "and which remained an important aspect of the Victorian culture of self-help until the coming of old age pensions and state health insurance schemes in the early twentieth century."

How did modern brass bands manage to get going in the villages of the Dales around 1860? The example of the Arkengarthdale band, as researched by Duncan Bythell, is illuminating. It was first referred to as a 'saxhorn band' in June, 1860, when it headed a procession to commemorate the dedication of a new harmonium in the parish church. It obviously relied on community support for such fund-raising efforts as the tea-party, concert, and dance which it organised at Langthwaite on 25 August, 1863.

In the later nineteenth century, various types of village bands were established. Drink versus anti-drink was one of the fundamental social and political divides within the local community. This division was very apparent in places like Hawes and Reeth where temperance and non-temperance bands co-existed. "Indeed," adds Duncan Bythell, "unless a band was specifically committed to the temperance cause, it seems to have been generally assumed that most of its members were involved to some degree in the 'culture of drink'."

My own special interest has been in the brass band contests at Hardraw Scar. It was in 1948 that moves were made to revive the brass band contests which had taken place here for years until they ceased in 1926, though occasionally the bandstand was used until it fell into disrepair. In the summer of 1934, the new Ingleton brass band gave a concert there in aid of Leeds Infirmary.

The revival occurred at Reeth through the enterprise of the Swaledale and Arkengarthdale Athletic Association. Old men began to recall the days when the valley below the Scar was 'black wi' folks'. The use of the gorge once a year by a committee of public-spirited people about Hawes, was permitted by the Earl of Wharncliffe, who owned the estate, living in some state at Simonstone Hall. The leading bands and choirs received substantial prizes.

About 1885, in the recollection of a Wensleydale man who used the pseudonym 'Ichabod', when he wrote to me at The Dalesman: "Father said: 'Now lads, bi sharp an' git all done. Weal go to Hardra' efter dinner. Put t'hoss into t'Shandra'." It was a tremendous day for the local liverymen, for there was no horse bus and various vehicles were used to transport the thousands of people who wished to avoid walking. "The roads were so crowded that I remember shouting, as we were about to get home: 'Look, Dad, John Moore of Yorescott is going the wrong way'. Dad replied: 'No, 'e's going round bi Appersett to save time'. The railway from Leyburn had not long been open and every available siding from Moorcock Station almost to Leyburn was filled with numerous trip trains."

Musicians from all parts of the North who arrived at Hawes railway station usually played through the main street before travelling on to Hardraw. Wagonettes had a busy time transporting the bands, choirs and hundreds of spectators drawn to Wensleydale on the great day. In the 1890s, the cost of a return rail ticket from Middlesbrough to Hawes was 1s.6d.

The bands competing in Victorian times included Black Dyke Mills, Besses o' the Barn and Kingston Mills. The compositions and excerpts selected as test pieces were often from classical operas. In 1898, the band test piece was Donnizetti's Overture to *Lucia di Lammermoor*. The male voices grappled with Blumenthal's *What Care I?*

The choirs sang in a clearing above Hardraw Force, with plenty of space for all. Looking down, the contestants could see the bandstand but could not hear a sound. The two contests therefore did not clash. The greatest natural disaster of recent times was a thunderstorm which occurred on July 12, 1899. The force of water ruined the old scaur and created a new course. The level at which the floodwater rose in the passage at the Green Dragon, in Hardraw, was pointed out for many a year afterwards. After the great flood the contests ended until, following the 1914-18 war, Edmund Blythe bought the grounds and made the Scaur safe for contests and crowds of spectators. He built the bandstand.

Dr J Sutcliffe Smith used to call Hardraw "the battlefield of bands", describing the setting in the narrow valley as "an ideal, ready-made open-air concert room, with an auditorium capable of holding 30,000 people, the like of which is probably not to be found elsewhere in Great Britain." Just as remarkable, in due course, was the necessity for visitors to first pass down the grey centre passage of the Green Dragon Inn, where at one time there was a fourpence entrance fee.

The decline of Hardraw's musical contests in the 1920s was blamed partly on the coming of t'wireless, which brought good music into almost every home. In 1927, only two bands competed. The revived band contest, using a substantial bandstand, with a grassy slope providing a natural auditorium, is today a major musical event in the Dales.

I have already mentioned the Lofthouse and Middlesmoor Silver Prize Band, who attend Tan Hill Show. When first I heard them play, they wore 'civvies'. It was in 1953, while visiting Nidderdale, that I heard of the genesis of this well-known Dales band. Tom Bradley, who had been mine host at the Crown Hotel for 46 years, told me he used to live at Carleton-in-Craven and played in both the Carleton and Skipton bands. He moved to Grassington and linked up with the village band.

It was natural, when he crossed Greenhow to settle in the upper valley of the Nidd that he should inquire about a band he might join. There was none—so, in 1914, he helped to start a band, which originally had 14 members. At the time I met him, Tom had ceased to play, though he served as conductor. ''I played the cornet for 62 years. Then the doctor told me that I had to stop it. It was doing me harm. So I gave up.''

Almost all the Dales bands were out busking at Christmas. Reeth Band, formed about 1859, was playing at Grinton one Christmas time when (records Margaret Batty) ''an old man whose generous nature far exceeded his pocket and grievously tried his wife, invited a number of the bandsmen to go into his house and have their dinner. Taking them in, he called out: 'Jane, is t'dinner readty? These men weean't want to wait, the'll etter git back playin'.'' Jane replied shortly: 'Whya taties ison, but fire's out'.''

The Giggleswick band travelled on the 7-10 a.m. train to Clapham on Christmas Day and called at the Flying Horse Shoe before walking up to the village. After playing at the squire's house, they were provided with a good breakfast. For the rest of the day, they toured the farms, including some at Austwick and Lawkland, and eventually arrived back home. By this time, the bandsmen had imbibed a great deal of liquid refreshment—the stuff that is stronger than lemonade—and were hardly capable of holding up their instruments, let alone of playing. John Walmsley Heelis, who told me about it, added: "So we burst into song instead!"

One year, when the band breakfasted before setting out on the Christmas round, they could not do justice to the hot punch bowl which was passed round at the Flying Horse Shoe. One of the men suggested they might take the punch with them. "Johnny—thee put it in thi' trombone, and we'll have a sup on t'rooad, but be careful ta hod it reight side up—an' doan't play." The trombonist did as he was commanded. The punch was disposed of by the men o' brass during the one and a-half mile walk from the railway station to the village of Clapham.

It was John Heelis who related what must be the strangest of the Dales band stories. The year after he played the bass trombone, he was asked to play the double bass. He did not know that the main tuning slide was loose. As he dashed for the train at Giggleswick, it fell out. The loss was not discovered until, at the Flying Horse Shoe beside Clapham station, the band began to play *Hail Smiling Morn*. No notes would come.

Mine host, hearing of their plight, suggested they have a look in the stables. Clapham Old Band, which was long defunct, used to practice there. "Sure enough," said John, "we found part of another instrument, but it proved too small." A bit of hosepipe was requested and this was fitted to the part which had been found. The slide was made to work.

"This contraption was in the Giggleswick band room for many years to remind the men of a particular Christmas visit to Clapham."

Choral Music

IN 1926, Jim Sidwell was a member of the Nelson Arion choir which competed in the male voice choir class at Hardraw Scar. They travelled in two motor coaches via Ingleton, and just beyond Newby Head, where there was a fine prospect of the fells around Widdale and Wesleydale, a halt was called for a pre-arranged rehearsal. The conductor tapped his tuning fork, gave each part its note and the choristers gave tuneful voices with the sweeping moors around them and the audience consisting of a few sheep.

For a Lancashire band competing at a festival held in Yorkshire, they could not have done better, winning the first prize, which was fifteen guineas in cash. Then, while one of the coaches returned to Nelson, the other crossed the Buttertubs Pass to Muker where John Richard Cooper, a native of the village, had arranged for choristers to give two concerts in the Methodist Chapel which, on each occasion, was packed to suffocation.

Overnight accommodation was arranged, Jim and his pal Wilf being billeted at a fellside farm, where their host was a pious man. He gave them plenty of food. When, on the Sunday, they inquired if he would sell them one of the small round cheeses which were popular, he replied: "Yo can 'ave one apiece, but yo'll 'ev to send t'brass on. Ah nivver trade on Sundays." As they set off for the Sunday concert, the farmer summoned the two men to a tryst at the back of the barn. He then whispered, as though afraid the Almighty might be listening: "Yo can pay fer them cheese. It'll save sendin' t'brass on."

Courting on Ilkla' Moor

1. Wheear 'as tha been sin' ah saw thee? On Ilk - ley Moor baht 'at.

OLICANIANS with a special regard for their elegant town did not take kindly to a ballad about a courting couple on the Moor and the possibility that the man, having gone without a hat and getting his death o' cold, might die, with consequences expressed in a way which was—well, er—a trifle vulgar. Who wants to think of being eaten up by worms which in turn will be gobbled down by ducks, which... You will know the rest.

Though not in pure dialect, Ilkla Moor reflects the pawky humour of the old West Riding towns. Easy to remember, and fun to sing, it is known round the world. I joined in singing it at a guest house at a remote spot in Iceland. A few Southerners had no difficulty in picking up the words and joining in.

Ilkla' Moor is said to have been written in 1886 when a Halifax church choir had a picnic on Ilkley Moor. Such an outing, from church or chapel, was popular on Whit Tuesday, being an excursion for grown-ups after the children had their annual procession, known as a walk, on the previous day. The usual form of transport was a wagonette. For church groups in the West Riding, Bolton Abbey or Ilkley Moor were firm favourites. Others plodded up from Eldwick, via Dick

Hudson's pub, and were soon exposed to "moorland breezes 'at scahr thi mind/Of all thi trouble and sorra'," as one poet wrote.

An old friend, T Wray Milnes, used to recall when he was one of those being bowled along in an old horse brake. It was then that the most familiar hymns and psalms were rendered as part songs, often with paradies, profane like *Ilkla Moor* or less profane like *Pratty Flowers*, the Holmforth anthem. He remarked: "Though not a folk tune, the combination of words and music thus widely disseminated in an oral tradition may properly be called a folk song," adding that perhaps they were the last of such northern 'wood notes wild' before the rising generations were overwhelmed by less edifying songs.

The Yorkshire ballad relates that a man and Mary Jane, the girl he loved, left the party for a time, engrossed in their happiness, to go courting. On their return, one of their friends wanted to know "Whear 'as ta bin sin' Ah saw thee?" The response was: On Ilkla' Moor baht 'at." The word baht is said to derive from the Anglo-Saxon butan, meaning outside of, without or except. In the case of the Victorian ballad, 'without' is the operative word. An old West Riding story relates that a visitor to Saltaire, seeing the sides of dray inscribed in yellow paint "Sir Thomas Salt, Bart, Sons and Company, Limited", remarked: "Well, in spite of all, Sir Titus 'ed 'is ups and darns i' life. He wore bart sons an' is company wor limited." 'At is, of course, 'hat' with the H dropped.

The song quickly and spontaneously developed into a song, and as the members of a church choir would turn naturally to hymn tunes, the tale of Mary Jane's young man (we do not know his name) was set to one called *Cranbrook*, composed by Thomas Clark in 1805. The most famous tune of this Canterbury cobbler was widely used in nonconformist psalmodies of the nineteenth century, sometimes to the hymn "Come ye that love the Lord" but more often to the carol "While shepherds watched their flocks by night", when the third line of each verse was sung twice and the last line repeated twice.

Cranbrook was much less used for worship when the song about Ilkla' Moor became popular. I recall taking a special service at Settle which stressed Yorkshireness. We sang with gusto about flock-watching shepherds to the old tune.

The second verse of *Ilkla' Moor* begins with the words "Tha's bin a-cooartin' Mary Jane." More verses were added later, suggesting that the capless individual was going to get his death of cold and giving a doleful prophecy of what would happen to him. Another local tale is that the tune was made up by one Amy Taylor, who was a dressmaker at Ilkley. She thought it up when working. Old residents of Ilkley, when asked about the song, could not remember it being sung locally until just before the 1914-18 war.

The words of the famous song are as follows:

> Wheear ha ta bin sin' ah saw thee?
> On Ilkla Moor baht 'at;
> Wheear 'as ta bin sin' ah saw thee,
> Wheear 'as ta bin sin' ah saw thee,
> On Ilkla' Moor baht 'at,
> On Ilkla' Moor baht 'at,
> On Ilkla Moor baht 'at.

Each verse is a similar repetition of words, the appropriate line for each of the next six verses being:

> Tha's bin a-coortin' Mary Jane.
> Tha's bahn ter ketch thi deeath o' cowd.
> (or "Tha'll go an' ketch thi death o' coed".).
> Then we shall ha ter bury thee.
> Then t'wurrms'll come an' ate thee up.
> Then t'ducks'll come an' ate up t'wurrms.
> Then we sall go an' ate up t'ducks.
> Then we sall all ha etten thee.
> Then we'll ha git us owan back
> (or "That's wheear we git us owan back").

After the fifth and sixth line of each verse, the bass voices of the chorus may interject an additional "'baht 'at".

An alternative version in the Ilkley Museum has the lines:

> Wheear wer to bahn w'en Aw saw thee?
> Aw wor a-coortin' Mary Jane.
> Aw'll tell thi mother/father w'en she/he comes whooam.
> Tha'll sewerly ketch thi deeath o' cowd.
> Then yo can coom an' berry me.
> Then wurrms'll coom an' ate thee oop.
> Ahr ducks'll gobble up the wurrms.
> An' yo can gobble up the ducks.
> An' so get back yer awn.

There is much about the song which remains mysterious, not least the identity of the song-writer and the name of the lad who went on t'moor baht 'at. Some people claim it was first written about another stretch of moor, one contender being Lindley Moor, on the outskirts of Huddersfield, but Ilkley has gone into the song-book, so contenders stand little chance of being adopted.

The *Ilkley Gazette* (1959) contained the following note: "A daily newspaper of immense circulation has been publishing correspondence about the meaning of 'baht 'at', thereby giving Ilkley some valuable publicity whilst revealing the ignorance of at least one of its readers. From an address in Twickenham, Middlesex, which possibly may explain his views, this reader delivers himself of the following pronouncement: 'The 'at' is not a hat but is the local pronunciation of 'ow', which means 'anything'. In other words, the chap concerned was on Ilkley Moor without his clothes." That was meant to explain why the song goes on to say that he would catch his death of cold!

Dick Hudson's, the hostelry at the moor-edge above Eldwick, had its own ditty, which was popular before the 1914-18 war. It was sung to the tune *Yip-i Addy I-hey* and went as follows:

When we get up there
We shall enjoy the Salt-aire
And fancy we're sat by the sea.
And if you are so willing
And I have a shilling
We'll call at Dick Hudson's for tea.
Yip-i Addy I-hey, etc.

Returning to Ilkla' Moor, I recall the early days of diesel trains on the Bradford-Skipton line, when a driver who was bored by his monotonous two-tone horn decided to 'hot up' the 'doh-fah' to 'doh-fah-fah-fah-doh-fah'. It sounded just like the tune for *Ilkla' Moor.*

Terrible Knitters 'e Dent

THE strangest musical sounds must have been that of the Dent hand-knitters as, sitting in the gloom of a local house, knitting and crooning away the evening hours, they sang:

> Bell-wether o' Barking, cries, baa, baa,
> How many sheep have we lost today?
> Nineteen we have lost, one have we faun'
> Run Rocky, run Rocky, run, run, run.

William Hewitt, in his book *The Rural Life of England* (1844), told us about this custom and the song is still rendered, while knitting, by Betty Hartley and Elizabeth Middleton, when demonstrating the old dales craft of hand-knitting. A bell-wether was a male sheep and Barking the name of a fell above Dent Town. Rocky was the dog of a shepherd. The knitter who sang this completed one round of a stocking. Then, at the beginning of the second round, it was sung again in modified form. Now it was 'eighteen we have lost, two have we faun' [found]." And so on...

I first saw Elizabeth in her Dales garb in 1976 when she appeared on the 'down' platform of Dent station, 1,100 ft above sea level, with others from the dale, when a special train of assorted historical coaches arrived to mark the centenary of the start of passenger traffic on the Settle-Carlisle railway. From the grey clouds came sheets of rain or hail. Someone offered me a free ice cream, which I declined with thanks. Elizabeth and Betty have delighted a large number of people by talking about and demonstrating the old knitting style, which is performed rapidly with an extra needle accommodated in a dagger-like knitting-stick tucked into a leather belt. The two ladies talk as they rock and then

The song "Tarry Woo'," as used by Betty Hartley
and Elizabeth Middleton.

croon their way through the production of a pair of socks or gloves.

Originally, the Dent knitters spun and used local wool. When there was not enough wool to go round, because virtually everyone was knitting, wool arrived from Kendal weekly, the same horse-drawn cart taking back to Kendal the finished products—among them stockings and gloves.

The definitive story of Dales hand-knitting was written for us at *The Dalesman* by Marie Hartley and Joan Ingilby, who are still drawing on their huge reserves of knowledge of Dales life in books and leaflets. The well-known phrase "the terrible knitters e' Dent", first appeared in a miscellany called *The Doctor*, the work of Robert Southey, in which he recounted in dialect the adventures of Betty and Sally Yewdale. As children, in about 1760, they were sent from Langdale in the Lake District to Dentdale to be taught how to knit. The word terrible in this context means 'great'.

The story, as told by Betty Yewdale, the oldest girl, was presented in the dialect of Dentdale. It tells how a Dent woman visited a neighbour of the Yewdales in Langdale, at the heart of the Lake District. Mr and Mrs Yewdale sent their two lasses back with her so they might 'larn' how to knit the Dent way. At the time, Betty was "between sebben an' eight year auld, an' Sally twea year younger."

They did not care much for Dent, though the local people made them welcome. The Lakeland girls were unaccustomed to the type of food supply, and especially the 'round Meal'. It was the local custom to "stoult it int' frying pan, e' keacks as thick as my finger." They were soon wearied of excessive knitting. They attended school, walking a mile each way to their lessons. "Maister an' Mistress larnt us our lessons, yan a piece—an' then we o' knit as hard as we cud drive, striving whillk cud knit t'hardest yan against anudder."

Betty recalled that the knitting of the Dent women was stimulated by singing a special song:

> Sally an' I, Sally an' I,
> For a good pudding pye,
> Taa hoaf wheat, an tudder hoaf rye,
> Sally an' I, for a good pudding pye.

When they got to the end of every needle, they called out the names of dalesfolk, which was easy for them. Sally and her sister got round the problem by using the names of folk back home in Langdale. They sang the song, altering the names at every needle, "and when we com at t'end cried 'off' an' began again an' sea we strave on o' t'day through."

Eventually the lasses, weary of the work and ignoring the fact that snow had fallen, sneaked away from their house, which was "four mile on 'todder side o' Dent's Town", and "axed t'way to Kendal...We poted alang leaving our lile footings behint us—we hed our clogs on—for we durstn't change them for our shoon for fear o' being fund out." After several adventures, the lasses returned home to a tearful re-union with their parents.

Marie and Joan researching the subject, were soon aware of how important was knitting to the local economy. Even before the enclosure of the Dent commons in 1859, there was so much ill-feeling and confusion about land use that a man might stay with his sheep overnight, to ensure they had good grazing. He had a small hut as shelter. What better than to pass the lonely hours knitting?

Old-time writers have left us some vivid word pictures of the days when hanks of rough, undyed wool were brought into Dent Town by packhorse (later, by the local carter), and finished items, which included caps, mittens, gloves and stockings, were taken out of the dale to be distributed for sale. Adam Sedgwick, who is commemorated by a great slab of Shap granite reared in the cobbled main street of Dent, wrote of distant times when a little local wool was retained and spun into a very coarse and clumsy thread; "and so it supplied the material for a kind of rude manufacture that went, I think, under the elegant name of Bump."

The dalesfolk later became familiar with finer material prepared by the woolcomber. Sedgwick wrote of the knitting schools "where the children first learnt the art many of them were to follow through life." We read of family parties assembling in one place on a winter evening and knitting by fire and candlelight. Such a gathering was sociable and saved fuel and candles. On the following evening, another home would be visited.

Sedgwick wrote nostalgically in 1868, when the 'sitting' was already old history. He recalled that "they took their seats; and then began the work of the evenings; and with a speed that cheated the eye they went on with their respective tasks. Beautiful gloves were thrown off complete and worsted stockings made good progress...There was no dreary deafening noise of machinery; but there was the merry heart-cheering sound of the human tongue."

William and Mary Howitt, who arrived in Dentdale in the 1840s, became aware of the curious posture of the hand-knitters. "They sit rocking to and fro like so many weird wizards...And this rocking motion is connected with a mode of knitting peculiar to the place, called swaving, which is difficult to describe. Ordinary knitting is performed by a variety of little motions, but this is a single uniform tossing motion of both the hands at once, and the body often accompanying it with a sort of sympathetic action."

Over the years, much of my information about hand-knitting has come from Betty Hartley and Elizabeth Middleton. Once, with a camera crew of Yorkshire Television, I interviewed the two ladies sitting in Elizabeth's home in the village. They were dressed in their eighteenth century knitting garb, with clogs on their feet and knitting in their hands. The TV story began with Betty walking along the cobbled street of Dent on her way to see Elizabeth. I can still hear the ringing of the iron-shod clogs on stone and recall the sideways glances by visitors when they saw this bonneted and be-shawled figure knitting as she walked.

Elizabeth was born at Deepdale Head. Members of her family had been knitters, but it was not until she met Betty and they discussed the old craft that she herself took it up. They were fellow members of the Women's Institute and inspired by research done by Kim Lyon into the knitting industry. Elizabeth showed me a chubby knitting-stick which had belonged to her grandmother, who before her marriage was an Allen. The initials E.T. were carved into another stick, representing the name Elizabeth Thwaite, who was an aunt. I was shown some old brass knitting needles, known as 'wires'; or 'pricks', which had belonged to Mrs Mabel Akrigg, of Weathercote Cottage. They, like the others I had seen, were slightly curved so that they could be used in conjunction with a knitting-stick. "Years ago," said Elizabeth, "when a couple were engaged, the young man would make her a knitting stick—a sort of love token."

Betty Hartley, who was born in 1913, is the fourth generation of her family to live in Cage Farm, Dent. Her grandmother was yan o' terrible knitters, sitting in a rocking chair, rocking incessantly and striking the loop with every 'rock'.

At that time, almost everybody knitted. "It was really an important part of the social life as well as a matter of earning part of their living."

When Betty was three years old, grannie encouraged her to knit. Betty has the leather belt with a buckle which her grandmother used when knitting. She has some striking examples of knitting sticks made by her grandfather, William Oversby, who was a cabinet-maker. The stick which he gave to his bride, and which he fashioned from ash, is also in her collection. For other sticks, he used wood from a pear tree and provided an inlay consisting of strips of brass and bone and Spanish mahogany.

From Cage Farm, we looked along the dale to the next building, Low Ground, now a holiday cottage, but once a dame-school where, among other subjects, knitting was taught to the children. "They went to read and write but, most importantly, to knit." Low Ground belongs to Betty, who explained: "We used to practice in the old dame-school in winter when there were no visitors. It was very suitable really." Knitting was not just a woman's occupation. At a time when farming was small-time, and when around a thousand people lived in the dale, it was vital to earn extra cash, so everyone in Dent—men, women and children—applied themselves to knitting.

I inquired about the 'knitting songs' and was told that at the 'sittings', knitters had entertained each other with tales and gossip. They also crooned songs which were not only tuneful; they were devised to stimulate them to maximum efforts when knitting. Such as:

> Bell wether Barking cries baa, baa, baa,
> How many sheep have we lost today?
> Nineteen have we lost, and yan [one] have we fun [found]
> Run, Rocky, run. Rocky, run, run, run,

The song, in conjunction with the knitting process, dealt with the loss and discovery of sheep in such a way that from the original disaster eventually none had been lost and all twenty were to hand. "At each verse, if a knitter was quick enough, she should be able to use the three needles to knit round the sock that was being made. And at the end of the song, the knitter should have finished twenty rows. That's very much quicker than Elizabeth Middleton and I can knit. The old songs were to encourage the knitters to get on." The old sheep-counting numerals—yan, tan, tethera, etc—were used and featured in particular in the song beginning: "Yan, tan, tethera, mi wark is niver done..."

Wool from local sheep still bore traces of the salve used to annoint the skins of the sheep in the previous November, when farmers 'shed' the fleeces, systemically separating lengths of wool in strips and applying the salve on a finger dipped into the salve-pot and then drawn along the bare skin of the animal, the body of which eventually covered with the noxious mixture. It was supposed to enable the sheep to winter well and to kill any keds or other insect pests. Salving was a nasty, tedious job. One sheep represented an hour of hard work in a stuffy outbuilding where work continued well into the night by the light of tallow candles. The hands of the salvers went jet-black.

Salved wool was tarry wool, hence the title of the old song which Betty and Elizabeth sing it at their regular demonstrations of knitting: Betty, interrupting her gardening on a bright morning in June, when the meadows were yellowed with buttercups and cumulus clouds drifted by like giant woolsacks, crooned her way through her favourite version of the music. One version of the words of *Tarry Woo'* are as follows:

> Tarry woo', tarry woo',
> Tarry woo' is ill to spin.
> Card it well, O card it well
> 'Ere you begin —
> When it's woven, dressed and clean,
> It will be clothing for a queen.

Sing ye bonny harmless sheep,
That feed upon the mountains steep.
Bleating sweetly as ye go
Through the winter's frost and snow.
Hart and hind and fallow deer,
Not be half so useful are.
Frae kings to him that hods the plough
Are all obliged to Tarry Woo'.

Up ye shepherds, dance and skip
O'er the hills and valleys trip:
Sing the praise of Tarry Woo'
And of the flock that bears it too—
Harmless creatures without blame,
They clothe the back and cram the wane.
Keep us warm and harty, too,
Weels on us our tarry woo'.

How happy is a shepherd's life.
Far fraw courts and free of strife.
While the gimmers bleat and bae
And the lambkins answer mae
No such music to his ear
Of thief or fox he has no fear.
Sturdy Kent and colly, too—
We'll defend the tarry woo'.

He lives content and envies none.
Not even a monarch on his throne.
Tho' he the royal sceptre sways,
Has not sweeter holidays.
Who'd be a king can only tell,
When the shepherd sings saw well—
Sings saw well and pays his due,
With honest heart and Tarry Woo'.

The Dent knitters needed to be 'terrible' because of the poor return on their work. Gloves in Fair Isle pattern brought a shilling a pair, even though the work included knitting a name into the pattern. Betty Hartley used to wonder how the old-time knitters found needles which were fine enough for

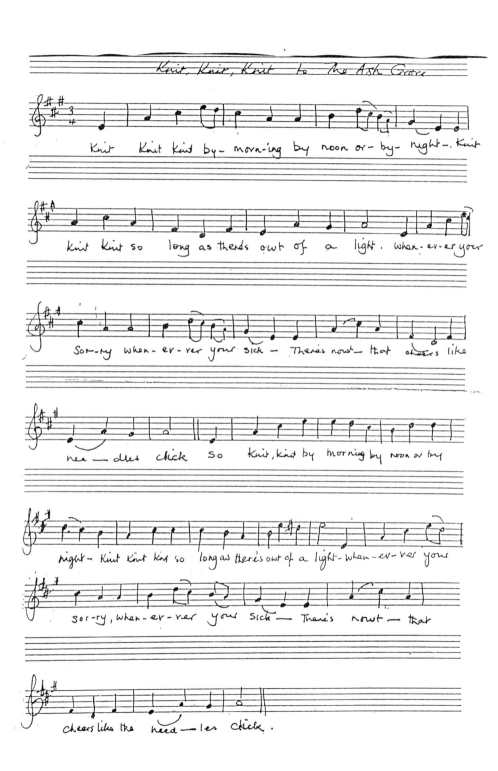

such work. She was told by one veteran that they were knitted on the old-style long hatpins.

Dent and Sedbergh, for centuries part of the West Riding of Yorkshire, have been in Cumbria since 1974 but the area still lies within the Yorkshire Dales National Park. The songs used have been long shared with Westmerians, one example being a song called *Knit, knit, knit,* which is sung to a traditional Welsh tune—*Ash Grove*. The song, which applies to the Dent knitters, and has been sung here for many years was rendered at the Mary Wakefield Festival in Kendal some sixty years ago.

The Dent choir of today is fond of singing English folk tunes. In the summer of 1997, by request, they assembled in the grounds of the Meeting House and sang for the guests at a Quaker wedding. And the two friends were looking forward to dressing up and demonstrating Dales knitting at the forthcoming Hawes Gala.

From a score by Ken Briggs, arranged by Mrs M Dutton.

Sacred Music

METHODISM was born in song. The followers of John Wesley were introduced to a form of worship in which choir-led singing was an important element. Their hymn book was virtually the Bible set to music. Methodism made a particularly strong appeal to the working class of the North, which included the lead-mining communities of the Dales, hence the particularly big chapels at Gunnerside and in Arkengarthdale.

Methodism, an outstanding ethical and educational force in the Dales for two centuries, is now but the proverbial shadow of its former self. Gone are the days when packed chapels reverberated to the singing of such mighty hymns as those written by the Wesley brothers, John and Charles, including the latter's

> Come, thou long-expected Jesus
> Born to set thy people free,
> From our fears and sins release us,
> Let us find our rest in thee.

Margaret Batty relates that when much of the preaching was by itinerants, they never forgot their times in the Dales Circuit. "It was notorious for unspeakable weather, damp beds and people so hardened that they never noticed either." Benjamin Rhodes was sent here in 1782. He is best remembered for his great hymn "My Heart and Voice I Raise to sing Messiah's Praise". At the time he was in the Dales, he was known among fellow-preachers as the author of the Itinerants' Anthem which, comments Dr Batty, "if not meritorious as poetry, is at least heart-felt":

O'er winter's bleak forests I roved
Or tried the impassable road:
With terrible dangers I strove
Then found a cold smokey abode.
A few hours there made my stay,
Then meeting the Tempest again
I weathered the cold winter's day
Exposed to the frost, snow and rain.

Dalesfolk used to rally to the Lovefeast, a joyous outburst of hymn-singing, testifying and the passing round of two-handled jugs of water from which each member sipped. The Lovefeast invariably began with Charles Wesley's hymn:

And are we yet alive, to see each other's face?
Glory and praise to Jesus give, for his redeeming grace.

Emotion ran high both at the Lovefeast and special Mission meetings at which conversions were hoped and prayed for. One worshipper is said to have been so overcome, he kicked out the back of the preceding pew. At Grassington, a woman—much moved by the fervour—stood up and said: "O Lord, tak my lad by his clogs and dangle him ower hell's fire." Then, remembering that the clogs were new, she added: "But nobbut give him a swither."

The Chapel at Gunnerside was built to hold about 500 people. Soon, with emigration, at a time when lead-mines were being closed, it was to be well-filled but once a year, on the first Sunday in July, when the Midsummer Festival draws back old residents and their families from the North-East and Lancashire towns. The annual Festival is still a notable annual occasion in Gunnerside and the dale, with special musical items from the Gunnerside Choir. A woman whose memories of girlhood include the Midsummer Festival remembers sitting up in the gallery and being impressed by the ladies of the choir. They sat in front of the organ, facing the congregation, dressed in their best finery, everyone having a decorative hat. "It seemed to be who could be the smartest. Now there is not a hat to be seen and fashions are more casual."

A service at 2 p.m. includes items from the children of Gunnerside School. The evening service begins with half an hour of hymn singing, from 6-00 to 6-30, led nowadays by David Rutter, who returns to his native village for this occasion. It is then that the hymn "O Love of God how Strong and True" is sung to the tune *Gunnerside*, composed by Jas Reynoldson. (Another of his compositions, a hymn tune entitled *Muker*, is played by Muker band and is sung in Swaledale to the hymn "Sweet is the work my God my King").

I have had several insights into the yearning of exiled dalesfolk for their old home. When I was invited to show some slides at a special fund-raising event at the Methodist Church in Colne, I shared the programme with one of the fine Lancashire choirs and was amazed at the large size of the congregation, many of whom were descendants of Swaledale families who had migrated to the East Lancashire textile belt on the failure of lead-mining.

At the Colne chapel, I was reminded that Francis Duckworth, composer of the hymn tune *Rimington*, had played the organ here for many years. Francis, a native of the village of Rimington, in the shadow of Pendle Hill, composed the famous tune to be sung to "Jesus Shall Reign Where'er the Sun". This made a strong appeal to those engaged in foreign missions and it was soon being sung throughout the Empire, which meant in effect the World. Several million copies were eventually in print.

The composer's musical life began when his family moved a short distance to Stopper Lane, taking over the village stores and post office adjacent to the Wesleyan Chapel, which was then the musical centre of the district. An orchestra and not an organ was used to accompany the hymn-singing. Bi-weekly practices were held at farmhouses, which in winter necessitated members of the orchestra travelling along dark and rutted country roads.

The inspiration to compose the hymn came in the shop one morning when Uncle John, a farmer, arrived to order his groceries. He chatted with Francis's father on the merits of hymn writers, having a special fondness for the older ones. He instanced Isaac Watts. "His admiration for Watts carried him away," Francis Duckworth was to recall. "Standing in the middle of the shop floor, he raised his hand with a mighty flourish and demanded attention from those present. Then, in a deep, eloquent voice, full of meaning and fervour, he recited the line 'Jesus Shall Reign where'er the Sun'. He repeated it in impassioned tones. 'Do you know what that means?' he asked. 'It means that everybody, everywhere, is going to accept Him. Ah! Watts had the conception. He said more in that one line than many of your modern verse writers say in a whole hymn'."

Francis added: "I shall never forget the look on his face as, with hand uplifted, he uttered his emphatic declaration." It made such an impression on his youthful mind he resolved that if he were to compose a tune, it would be to that great hymn. Francis took organ lessons, and the organ eventually displaced the orchestra at Stopper Lane. When still a young man, he moved to Colne, thriving as a grocer. He became deputy organist at the Albert Road Methodist Church and played there for more than forty years. His tune *Rimington* was sung for the first time in the Colne Whitsuntide processions in 1904.

The tune known as *Bolton Abbey* was originally composed by George Bett Blanchard, who was choirmaster of Waltham Street Methodist Church, Hull, during a choir outing to Bolton Abbey, in Wharfedale. It was intended as a solo in which the hymn *Rock of Ages* was to be used as a chorus.

The old-style Dales chapel was box-like and unadorned, except for the Biblical text writ large on the wall behind a pulpit, which in size and importance was like the bridge of a ship, the rostrum supporting a family-size Bible. The pews were hard—harder still, after a twenty-minute prayer or a forty-minute sermon. The hymns were lustily sung, to the accompaniment of harmonium or small organ, which years ago was hand-pumped, a piece of lead, dangling on a string, being the pumper's guide as to how much air remained in the bellows.

Methodists like a good sing, especially to a familiar tune. Malcolm Skidmore, well-known throughout the Dales as an auctioneer, told of the preacher who, hearing unfamiliar strains from the harmonum, said to the lady organist: "Can we have a more up-to-date tune?" She replied: "You can't have anything more up-to-date than this. I'm makkin' it up as I goes on." The new book *Hymns and Psalms,* which is about brick size and weight, is not yet used in all the chapels. A steward asked me about it, smiled and remarked: "They tell me it's a block-and-tackle job."

For many years, until the 1914-18 war, Swaledale had a special funeral dirge. Details of it, complete with score, were collected by the Barker family and used by Margaret Batty in a booklet, *Gunnerside Chapel and Gunnerside Folk,* which was published in 1967 and sold for the benefit of chapel funds. A local lady, Elizabeth Rutter, recalled hearing the Dirge at a funeral and being "terrified by the doleful sound."

> Thee we adore, Eternal Name,
>   And humbly own to Thee
> How feeble is our mortal frame,
>   What dying worms we be.
>
> The year rolls on and steals away
>   The breath that first it gave.
> Whate'er we are, whoe'er we be,
>   We're travelling to the grave.
>
> Farewell, dear friends, a long farewell,
>   For we shall meet no more,
> Till we are raised with Christ to dwell
>   On Canaan's happier shore.

Margaret Batty related that the first two verses of this dirge came from a hymn by Isaac Watts, which was No 42 in *Wesley's Collection of Hymns for the Use of People called Methodists*, published in 1780. She could not trace the origin of the last verse. Tradition insists that this musical fragment 'dates from the monks'. The words do not, though the tune may be of great antiquity, one theory being that it was used in the Middle Ages by those who carried bodies in wicker coffins along the Corpse Way from the upper dale to Grinton. It subsequently acquired its eighteenth century phraseology.

Margaret Batty heard from the great-granddaughter of a local man, William Coates, that as he lay ill in bed, he heard a funeral procession coming down the other side of the valley. They were singing the Dirge out of tune. So he got up and shouted the correct version out of his window. "He was a man to be reckoned with."

James Reynoldson, composer of the hymn tunes *Muker* and *Gunnerside*, was prominent in church work and, recalls Jim Calvert, of Gunnerside, "was my Sunday School teacher. He was a small, cheery-faced man, always pleasant and obviously clever at composing."

My own love of song evolved largely through a Methodist upbringing at a large chapel in Skipton where the emotional heights were reached with the pre-Christmas performance of *Messiah*. Several hundred voices introduced *Messiah* with the singing of a joyous Christmas hymn, *O Come, All ye Faithful*. Several hundred worshippers analysed virtually every note sung by the soloists and later commented on any departures from orthodoxy. Woe betide anyone who sang too quickly, too slowly, too softly, too loudly or added what one old lady called 'twiddly bits' and were closer in style to Handel's work than the modern rendering.

There was also in Skipton an outstanding soprano, Elizabeth Harwood, whose singing enhanced many a concert and special service and who went on to achieve an international reputation as an opera singer. She was to recall singing

Wigglesworth.

7.6. 7.6. D.

ALICE FAWCETT

Price 3d

One of the many splendid hymns with a dale-country connection.

her first *Messiah* when, at the age of sixteen, she fulfilled an engagement which her soprano mother, Constance, was unable to keep because she had a bad cold. The performance was at a village near Skipton and Elizabeth was to receive a fee of one guinea. She was given 25s because she 'showed a lot of promise'.

Elizabeth Harwood grew up in a musical home. Her father, Sydney, was the Clerk of the old Skipton Rural District Council, which took in a large part of the Craven Dales. He was also a fine tenor. Elizabeth Harwood was to recall the 1939-45 war partly because it was a time when, growing up, she enjoyed Sunday evenings at home because they were devoted to singing in the old Edwardian tradition. Elizabeth joined the Northern College of Music in Manchester, where she had outstanding teachers to launch her on an exceptional career which ended—for her and a host of admirers—with her death at an early age.

When my old friend Don Mosey interviewed her for a book he was writing with Fred Trueman, she told him that many of the memories she treasured were of Yorkshire and the warm-hearted Yorkshire folk. She also loved the seclusion of being alone. Whenever she went back home, to Ilkley, she was impelled to visit the Cow and Calf Rocks at the edge of the moors. "It's sheer therapy and nothing can take its place."

Now and again, even in these ungodly times, I have had a glimpse of the old-time emotional as well as spiritual intensity of a Chapel service. Dalesfolk still enjoy a good sing at a funeral, especially if the dear-departed has had farming associations, for there are two classes of folk in this world—Farmers and Others.

Ted's funeral service was charged with emotion. It took place at a 'mission' chapel. Half an hour before the service, the vicinity of the chapel was packed with cars. By the time the service began vehicles lined either side of the road through the village while the owners, wearing crow-black clothes, thronged t'chapil, regarding the event as much a display of farming solidarity as a funeral.

The organist was power-assisted; she played one of the modern electric organs, with stereo. She was competent and yet only her fingers and feet moved. This was t'chapil, not a dance hall. We sang "The strife is o'er, the battle done". It began a little uncertainly but quickly gained power and assurance, with the exhaled breath during the last verse making the windows reverberate. "Lord, by the stripes which wounded Thee,/From death's dread sting Thy servants freee..." It was stunning!

A little man spoke with a resounding voice—like the outpourings of the diminutive jenny-wren. The form of the service was apparent—a repetition of Biblical text and cliques, non-stop, at the same pitch; a veritable wash of words, bringing responsive grunts or Amens from the faithful. We had another hymn—"When peace, like a river, attendeth my way..." It was a hymn full of Victorian certainty, with a refrain in which the congregation delighted: "It is well...with my soul...It is well, it is well with my soul." The delivery was slow, measured but—*vibrant!*

The address was homely, with a mention of Ted's aptitude as a farmer. But he was, above all, a lover of God. Ted's house was next to the chapel, which had been a do-it-yourself job. He would vault over the wall to do various practical jobs about the place. Although quite old, he had been known to lift a stone, resting it on his shoulder as he took it to where others were working. With the third hymn—"For ever with the Lord"—the congregation was in good voice. Then Ted's mortal remains were interred beside those of his late wife. Ted's spirit was, that day, in Paradise. That's what Ted believed. That's what Dales Methodism believed. And that's what the pastor had said, time and again, to attendant grunts and Amens from the faithful. Who were we to dispute it?

Composed by R Barrett Watson (1904) for the organ
of St Alkelda's, Giggleswick.

The Organ-builder

IN THE churchyard at Kildwick is a novel tombstone. It
takes the form of an organ, the first instrument to be
made by John Laycock, a noted local organ-builder.
John, born on November 24, 1809, at Cook House, Glusburn,
had little formal education and began work as a handloom
weaver, becoming a cartwright. It was not until his 30th year
that he became an organ-builder.

He had acquired the old organ of Ickornshaw Wesleyan
Chapel. He examined it, took the organ to pieces and
reconstructed it. Then he made an instrument of his own,
which he sold imediately to James Hartley of Glusburn. As
orders came in, Laycock switched from making carts to
organs. John Laycock, a tall, powerful man, was so impressed by organ music that he thought nothing on a Sunday of
walking to Leeds to attend a service at the parish church
when the organist was Dr S S Wesley. He responded to any
mechanical problem which came his way, making clocks, one
of them entirely of wood and indicating the hour of the day
and also the day of the month.

Three Musical Celebrities

Frederick Delius

YOU may have seen Ken Russell's film about Delius—a film based on Eric Fenby's book, *Delius as I Knew Him*. This was about the composer in his later days —blind, paralysed, with a grey and haggard look, reclining in a shady room, cheating the intense heat and light of summer at Grez in France. It is fascinating to think of two Yorkshiremen, an old but still spirited Delius and young Fenby, his amanuensis, who made it possible for the composer to record yet more work, and of 'Jelka' Rosen, a German painter, whom Delius had married in 1903.

And what music! Shimmering strains, evocative of sunlight falling on quiet landscapes; haunting passages evoking the spirit of high and lonely hills and of the sea; echoes in music of the New World, of Indians and Negro slaves heard by Delius when he was living in Florida, his first truly great adventure after breaking free from his West Riding family. Through his compositions, Delius was to blend the musical idioms of Europe and North America.

Somewhere in that rich and varied musical output was a thread relating to his native Yorkshire. The man who enjoyed turning his face towards the sun—who was, indeed, a January child, born in workaday Bradford, the wool capital of the world—enjoyed boyhood jaunts on the moors which provide Bradford with a ragged fringe, dark for most of the year but putting on a purple robe when the heather flowers in late summer.

Delius's greatest opera, *A Village Romeo and Juliet*, is set in hill country and contains as a glorious interlude *The Walk to the Paradise Garden*, which must run close second in popularity to his *On Hearing the First Cuckoo in Spring*. How much of his native Yorkshire—of the moors and dales—is to be found in the work of a composer whose music, rich in melancholy, conveys impressions of places he had visited? Delians like to think that there is a Yorkshire flavour.

The composer used to say, in a broad accent he never lost despite a long sojourn in France: "Let the critics say the work breathes my native Yorkshire, I never heard sleigh bells...in Bradford, but plenty in Norway and Sweden, and actually the wind will 'sough' almost anywhere...still, it's a nice thought!" Edvard Grieg, his friend since student days in Leipsig, described Delius as "this English-American, deeply musical, splendid Hardangervidde-man. He is like us in nothing except feeling! But in the end that's everything."

The Dales connection was brought out by his niece, Margaret de Vesci, daughter of Claire, his favourite sister, who wrote a piece which I gratefully accepted for *The Dalesman*. She noted that Delius had ridden a pony across Il-kley Moor and had swum in the Wharfe. He loved the grandeur of the dale-country and the characterful folk who inhabited it. Margaret, who had lived in the Delius household in France, helped her mother with the book *Memoirs of My Brother, Frederick Delius*, in which mother, who had a home in the Bronte Country, related how Delius brought his just-completed score of *Koanga*, for her opinion.

It was while staying in this moor edge district that he and Claire rode over the moors on horseback to look at Wuthering Heights. Delius even discussed with her the possibility of making Charlotte Bronte's *Jane Eyre* into an opera. Claire and her brother rode on horseback to Skipton Castle, the home of the Cliffords and Vesci's, into whose family Margaret was to marry. At Barden Tower, once the home of The Shepherd Lord (Clifford), they discussed astrology and his lordship's search for the Philosopher's Stone. Clifford had written on natural philosophy. So did Delius. In 1889, he produced a treatise on the effect of notes and pitches in music on the human body.

Delius was a Bradfordian with German parents. Julius Delius, an immigrant, presided over a wool-related company. Elise, his wife, was from the same part of Germany. Both became British citizens. They had fourteen children and Frederick, who was officially named Fritz Theodor Albert, was the fourth child. (Fritz was changed to Frederick). Side by side with Julius's business life went a range of cultural activities. He was a concert-goer who delighted in welcoming musicians to his home.

Frederick grew up hearing much good music and, clad in a velvet suit, he was sometimes brought down to play the piano for guests. At other times, he quit the city streets for the high hills, "leaving littleness behind in the low vales, where little cares are great." Young Delius was fond of trudging through heather or along sheep trods, under a big Pennine sky. He often stood quite still, for minutes on end, inspired by lovely sounds and scenes. The sights and sounds of the Yorkshire moors fed his imagination and he was fond of recalling them.

His parents rented a house on the outskirts of Ilkley for the summer holidays. They were also fond of staying on the Yorkshire coast, where Frederick would hear the gulls calling stridently above the boom of the sea. He was passionately fond of cricket and, at Scarborough, watched the exemplary batting of W G Grace. Frederick cut loose from the shackles of the family firm. His father set up his wayward son as an orange-grower in Florida and Frederick sailed there in 1884. He had little interest in the job.

Father supported his son financially while he had a musical education in Leipsig. Delius didn't care much for this but became friendly with Edvard Grieg and other Scandinavians. It was Grieg who persuaded Julius Delius that his son might have a worth-while career in music. An early composition, *On the Moors,* was influenced not by the tousled landscape of the West Riding but by Norway, via Ibsen. So was *On the Summit,* the first of his orchestral work to be performed in public, the occasion being a concert at Monte Carlo in 1893.

His tone poem entitled *Over the Hills and Far Away* was first performed publicly in London in 1899. It was the beginning of a twenty year period of composition which included his finest writing. He set to music poems by Arthur Symonds, including these words, which were not written about the Yorkshire moors but could apply to them:

> Bleating, a dog barks, at a farm in the vale;
> Blue thro' the bracken, softly enveloping
> Silence, a veil.

In 1912, Delius completed *Song of the High Hills,* for a wordless chorus and orchestra. It received its first English performance in 1920. Geoffrey G Hoare, who studied the life and work of Delius intensely, wrote in *The Dalesman* that it is "full of spacious solitude and far and wide horizons." *North Country Sketches,* completed just before the outbreak of the 1914-18 war, has a Yorkshire feel about it, even though it was not written in the county. Florence Foster Brook, "a hundred per cent Dales born and bred," treasured a recording of this composition and told me in 1962 that it transported her instantly to "my native hills, moors and valleys."

Delius liked to re-visit Yorkshire, which he did periodically during the 1914-18 war, when he and his wife lived for a time in England. In 1918, while staying near Skipton, he had an idea he might compose an opera based on *Wuthering Heights.* During his last debilitating illness, he was fond of recalling his Yorkshire boyhood, and in particular the stone setts in a Bradford street, steam trams, cricket and the hardy folk of the Dales. When Eric Fenby came to live with him and attempted to set down what little the composer could dictate, Delius said: "Imagine we are sitting in the heather, on the cliffs by the sea." Thus began *A Song of Summer,* in which he possibly was picturing boyhood holidays spent on a breezy cliffscape on the North Yorkshire Coast.

Delius, aged sixty-two years, had been awarded the Freedom of Bradford, being much moved when the Mayor, the Town Clerk and Mace Bearer of the city visited Grez to present him with a scroll. He died in 1934 and was buried at Grez-sur-Loing, France, where he had lived for thirty years. Among the wreaths (which arrived too late for the funeral) was one 'composed' of heather and other moorland plants which had been sent by the Mayor and citizens of Bradford.

Delius had expressed a wish to be buried in an English churchyard, so his mortal remains were moved, inexplicably, to Limpsfield, on the Surrey-Sussex border. Why not Yorkshire? His wife, having contracted pneumonia on the journey from France, and dying two days later, was buried in the same grave.

Roger Quilter

Q UILTER (1877-1953), whose compositions evoke the the spirit of Edwardian days, sprang from a Suffolk family and spent most of his life in London, where he became a celebrated composer, his best work being produced in the twenty years from 1905. He composed music settings for no less than ninety-seven songs.

In his later days, after the 1939-45 war, Quilter was introduced to Settle and North Ribblesdale by his valet, Harry Heaton, a native of Giggleswick who was the son of a platelayer employed on the Settle-Carlisle railway. Ada, Harry's wife, was a Nuttall from Settle, her family living at Rose Cottage, the old lodge for the Ashfield Hotel (now a social club) which was separated from the big house in the 1870s by a railway embankment. Roger Quilter's home in St John's Wood had been peppered by shrapnel from anti-aircraft guns and in London food was severely rationed. He must have rejoiced at the comparative quietness of the Dales and at the somewhat easy approach to food rationing in these parts.

Quilter had a special friendship with Jack Brassington and his family, to the extent that he sent them copies of his music, some in manuscript, signed Roger, and offering them good wishes. Older residents of Settle recall Roger Quilter walking about town, and especially an encounter he had with Jimmy Easter in Haygarth's cycle shop in Duke Street. As he walked into the shop—an impressively tall man, but with a voice which was soft and cultured—the somewhat brash Jimmy said: "In thy honest hopinion, which is t'best musical instrument?" Quilter, politeness itself, replied: "I don't know, Mr Easter...On reflection, I would say it was the violin." Jimmy triumphantly retorted: "Tha's wrong, tha knaws—it's trombone." Charlie Lawson, who worked for Haygarths for many years, was asked by the musical Jimmy if he had "dragged t'orchestra down in't muck." Charlie put a re-assuring hand on Jimmy's shoulder and said: "*No* Jimmy, tha didn't. They were already in't muck. Thou just dragged 'em about in it."

Not many of the residents of Settle would be aware of Quilter's considerable success as a composer. After three years at Eton, he had joined three other composers—Percy Grainger, Cyril Scott and Balfour Gardiner—at Hocks Conservatoire in Frankfurt. His forte was to become the drawing room song, usually based on such classical sources as Shakespeare, Herrick and Tennyson. It was Tennyson who provided the poetic setting for the hauntingly beautiful *Now Sleeps the Crimson Petal.*

The finest of his choral compositions, *Non Nobis Domine,* was given an airing at Settle in 1997, being among the Songs for a Summer Evening rendered by the Colne Orpheus Glee Union. The composer's best-known orchestral work, a jaunty *Children's Overture,* based on nursery rhymes, was originally written as the prelude to the incidental music for the children's play entitled *Where the Rainbow Ends.* Discarded, it was re-developed as a stand-alone overture.

Now for a little more of the local associations. Dennis Heaton, a nephew of Harry, frequently visited his relatives at the flat in St John's Wood and recalled Quilter as "always a gentleman." He was "tall, quite hefty, with silvern hair and a gentle, cultured voice." How did this shy, gangling, talented bachelor come to be associated with the Yorkshire Dales? He came North with the Heatons.

Quilter did not care much for physical exercise, so it was not the prospect of walking up hill and down dale. He was beset from childhood with stomach problems and was finicky about food, so roast beef and Yorkshire pudding were not the attractions. Quilter was prone to periods of anxiety about aspects of his personal life. He worried a lot. This cultured man, who could be easily moved to tears by an experience of good art, especially poetry and painting, appears to have enjoyed the several visits he paid to the Dales. He liked genuine people, and there were plenty of them at Settle.

Heads would turn with disbelief as Quilter sauntered through the town, clad in his city-type suit with a fawn waistcoat. Jack Brassington, one of the partners in a local joinery enterprise, was a specially good friend of the visiting composer. Jack described Quilter to me as "tall and quite hefty, but with a gentle voice." He added: "You might call him a Gentle Giant." Quilter's best days as a composer were over. Inwardly, he was often in turmoil, so the Heatons, with their no-nonsense Yorkshire background, would served him well. They in turn had status and pleasurable experiences, such as accompanying Quilter to the theatre or on cruises to exotic lands. He visited Settle at a time of post-war austerity and petrol rationing. The small party, completed by Quilter's dog and cat, travelled by train.

Harry and Ada stayed with Ada's relatives. Quilter was given accommodation on his first visit at *Hazel Dene,* in Stackhouse Lane, which was the home of Fred Pilkington, the owner of a local shoe shop where in their young days the Heatons had been employed. Quilter was photographed with Harry and Ada in garden settings. He was invariably seated, with drooping head, as though trying to offset his taller-than-average form.

It was Fred Pilkington who introduced the distinguished visitor to Jack Brassington, whose family had for many years owned a joinery establishment at Bridge End, Settle. Jack was a prominent member of the Settle Amateur Operatic Society and, having a fine tenor voice, often played the lead in productions of Gilbert and Sullivan. Quilter, lamenting the fact that there was no piano in the Pilkington household, was taken to the Brassington home on The Mains, where a good piano was available.

Jack was to recall: "He used our piano on many occasions during his first and second visits to Giggleswick. He was never happy unless he was putting notes to paper." Doris Brassington remembers him as spending a good deal of time making minor adjustments to a score. She asked Quilter if he would like a cup of coffee. He preferred a squashed banana and brown sugar. So that is what he had. Quilter accompanied Jack Brassington on a visit to the domed chapel of Giggleswick School on its gritstone crag above the famous public school, which Jack had attended. His father had done the joinery work when the chapel was built, at the expense of the millionaire Walter Morrison, to commemorate the diamond jubilee of Queen Victoria.

On his first visit, however, Quilter had the company of Harry Heaton and they arrived as the day's cleaning had just ended. The cleaner, Thomas Thistlethwaite, of Austwick, was a bluff, ruddy-faced, cheerful man known far and wide as 'Tommy Apple'. Tommy spent so much time gossiping with Quilter he forget he had made a heap of dust which was yet to be cleared and that he had temporarily left the sweeping brush on the altar. The brush was still there when the communion service began. Harry recalled: "We gave Tommy half a crown; he was suited to death."

Quilter subsequently inquired about the characterful Tommy Apple, being fascinated by his manner and deeds. Writing to Jack Brassington from his London home on April 25, 1952, a year before his death, Quilter recalled a recent visit by Jack and added: "I wish you did not live so far away. I really must try to come North later on. Do tell me Tommy Apple's real name and address, if you know it."

During his 1951 visit, the composer stayed at the Black Horse, Giggleswick. Writing to Jack Brassington from the Royal Ascot Hotel on September 20 of that year, he hoped that all was going well with Jack and his family and apologised because though he had stayed quite near to Jack's home, the chance of seeing him had not arisen. "It was delightful meeting you the time before, when I was staying at the Black Horse. Do you remember, you sang to me outside [the inn] one of my songs. I think it was *To Daisies*?"

Quilter, plainly much moved by the people he had met at

Settle, and especially by the kindness of the Brassington family, who gave him friendship and the use of their piano, sent them copies of his songs, either in manuscript or printed form, in the years 1951 and 1952. One, inscribed to Helen, their young daughter, was of the song A Good Child, from *Four Child Songs,* to words by Robert Louis Stevenson. The composer signed himself Uncle Roger. He forwarded printed music from *Where the Rainbow Ends.* He autographed copies of *Wild Cherry* and *Hark! Hark! The Lark.*

A further Settle connection was Quilter's friendship with Annice Haygarth (née Sidwell) and her husband, who were musical. Annice had an outstanding voice which was heard in local operatic productions and which got the best out of new songs by Quilter, who visited her home and provided the piano accompaniment. He also wrote to Annice about his current work.

Quilter spent part of his later life at Eagle House, St Andrew's Hospital, in Northampton, an expensive haven for those who had mental illnesses. While he was here, his finances plunged. In acknowledging a letter he had received from Annice, he added: "I must see what the Doctor says before I return home again." He invariably mentioned his ill-health in correspondence. "I assure you, I don't feel old at all. I am so glad you have been having music with Miss Aked and Mr Claughton. I have made such good friends through my music; that is always a great joy to me." Quilter asked Annie to find out if any hymns and choruses of his would be useful at Giggleswick School. "I will order one or two songs which you may not know from the publishers—and perhaps you might pass on some to Miss Aked." The composer ended his letter with best wishes to Annice, her husband and the two musical friends.

The association between Quilter and the Heatons is the key to the composer's association with the Yorkshire Dales. Harry and Ada first met each other when they worked for Fred Pilkington, who had shoe shops at Settle, Clitheroe and

Eastbourne. Mrs Pilkington kept the Black Horse at Gig-gleswick and Ada helped her here and also at the Gamecock, Austwick, when this was acquired. Harry Heaton, going to London to improve himself, became a valet and eventually came into the service of Roger Quilter.

A niece of the Heatons and her husband, who were newly married, visited Quilter's flat in St John's Wood, London, met the composer and had a meal here. She recalls that when he entered the room, they found his height somewhat intimidating, though he was gentle in manner and speech. The meal prepared by Aunt Ada is recalled mainly because it included asparagus, which the visitors had not seen before. Uncle Harry was dashing about, as was his wont. Quilter's orchestral works, on gramophone records, were being played quietly in the background.

I had already spent some years on research into Quilter's connections with Settle when I heard for the first time from several local people of his intention to live in the town.

When the time came for Harry and Ada to retire, they naturally wished to return to their native district. Quilter, who was not only dependent on the Heatons but appears to have had a real fondness for them, seems to have harboured thoughts of buying a house at Settle in which the dependable routine of St John's Wood might continue as before.

Early interest was shown in a roomy house on the southern side of the town but it was already claimed by a local family. In the event, Quilter died before a house was purchased. Subsequently, in September 1953, Harry bought Bond End, a detached house formerly connected with Marshfield, the dower house of the Dawsons of Langcliffe.

This property had been occupied by Miss Kathleen Wray, whose principal hobby was photography. She extended an already large house to provide a dark room in which to process her photographic equipment. She had a relatively large staff, four of whom, including two maids, were kept on sparse rations. Sometimes they cooked half a rabbit, which had to provide a meal for four people, including the two maids.

Bond End was requisitioned for evacuees during the 1939-45 war and was then occupied by people who spent little time or money on its maintenance. It was not in especially good order when Harry Heaton secured it. When Ada died, Harry moved to a terraced house in High Hill Grove Street, where paintings, furniture and artefacts which had belonged to Roger Quilter had an incongruously cramped setting.

Presumably, the mortgage on Bond End was cleared when he received his inheritance from the estate of Roger Quilter in the following March, for Harry was left £5,000, which was real wealth to one who hitherto had modest means. Harry also acquired most if not all of the contents of Quilter's flat in London.

After Harry's death, the oval painting featuring nudes which had hung above the fireplace in Quilter's flat in London, and subsequently occupied the same place above the small coal fire in Harry's diminutive home, was examined by a representative of Sotheby's, who found that the painting had little value, having been cracked and distorted through the long years by the blast of hot air from the coal fire immediately beneath it.

A fragment of music among scores sent to Jack Brassington is the last part of *Music and Moonlight,* which Quilter composed to words by Shelley. It is signed by the author. A musical appreciation of Quilter and the score is provided by Valerie Langfield, who has studied the composer's life and work intently. "Quilter was a meticulous composer, and a superb craftsman, refining a song, re-shaping it here and there, until he was happy with it. He produced most of his best work before he was 40; but this song, written when he was 57, is a gem from his later years.

"Now, there was always great detail in Quilter's writing, even in the final version of his songs, and in the original versions there was still more. It is fascinating to compare this

23 Acacia Road
London N.W.8.

April 25th 1952

Dear Jack

It was so nice seeing you, but
your visit was all too short!
I hoped I might have a little line
from you, to say how you all were and
if you all arrived home safely.
So just send a word to reassure me.
I can't remember if I gave Helen
a copy of "Where the Rainbow Ends"
music. Anyhow will you give her
this with my love!
I wish you did not live so far away —
I really must try & come North later on.
Do tell me "Tommy Apples" real name
and address, if you know it —
my love to you all, dear Jack!
always your affectionate friend

Roger.

A letter written by Roger Quilter to Jack Brassington of
Giggleswick on April 25, 1952. 'Tommy Apples' was the
nickname of Tommy Thistlethwaite, a local character.

manuscript score with the published version. In the manuscript (dated January 1935) there are a number of small ornaments and various extra notes for the pianist that, sure enough, in the final version, he has omitted. Why did he take out notes? Quite simply, to make the music easier to play. Quilter was always keen to keep his music accessible to as many people as possible, and so he took out some of the fiddly notes and altered the piano part so the hands move around less. His piano accompaniments always 'lie' well under the hand, and likewise the vocal line always sits well in the voice.

"*Music and Moonlight* is an atmospheric, delicate song. The accompaniment, with its half-strummed chords, gives hints of a guitar, while the melody floats on top. It is—unusually for Quilter—in a flowing 6/8 time. It is a setting of Shelley's poem The keen stars were twinkling, and the final words are typical of the sentiment that inspired Quilter; that 'music and moonlight and feeling are one'."

Edward Elgar

I HAVE dealt fully with Edward Elgar's association with the Dales in my book *Mr Elgar and Dr Buck; a Musical Friendship,* published by Castleberg (1991). Lady Barbirolli, who provided a foreword, wrote that the close friendship with Buck came at a valuable time for young Elgar—"just when he wanted the understanding of a trusted and caring friend to give him the confidence and the encouragement he so greatly needed."

They met at Worcester in 1882, when Buck was attending a British Medical Association conference and Elgar, then virtually unknown outside his native area, was charged with providing an orchestra for a soiree on the final day. Elgar was anxious to augment his little orchestra and a mutual friend  recommended that Buck, of Giggleswick, should be invited to bring his 'cello and take part.

Each discovered in the other a love for the countryside, for animals, especially dogs, and for music. Their friendship was to last almost exactly fifty years. Elgar paid several visits to Giggleswick. The two young bachelors walked, talked, played golf, undertook japes or 'jests' and, of course, gathered with friends in the evening to play music, usually in a fug of pipe smoke. One of the main rooms at Buck's house had a slide built into the upper part of the door. This was drawn back to allow the fug to disperse.

Elgar met Buck at a time when he was undecided which course his musical life should take. Should he continue as a musician or concentrate more on composition? The matter and others of a highly personal nature—such as his lost-love, Helen Weaver—were aired during walks in the district, especially along Giggleswick Scars. He enjoyed the austere beauty of the limestone country, the thunder of waterfalls and "a whiff of pure mountain air."

On visits to Giggleswick, he found time to compose, one early piece being *Rosemary*, originally a piano solo. He was also moved to write a scherzo. It is thought that Elgar, while at Giggleswyke, as he often called it, found time to polish up *Salut d'amour*. Music composed during what Percy Young has called Elgar's "long obscurity" was handled casually, as implied by a letter from Elgar to Buck: "I never had your mouldy Trio; I wrote for you a Minuet and Trio but that's all I ever remember doing & You must have it now somewhere."

Words by Col. John Hay were set to music at Giggleswick in August, 1885, creating typical ballad music of the time, and well suited to the Victorian love of gathering round a piano on Sunday evening to make music. The first verse goes as follows:

> Thro' the long days and years
> What will my lov'd one be
> Parted from me?
> Thro' the long days and years!

It has been suggested that this sad song was for a sad occasion—a break between Helen Weaver and Elgar, who was infatuated with her. Buck's copy of the song had the name Jack Baguley written upon it. Jack was a friend of the two men who had died through an accident while visiting

South America.

Elgar's local compositions were for a short time my property, having been given to me by one who had inherited the possessions of Monica Buck. I gave them to the Elgar Foundation and they now recline in the Birthplace Museum near Worcester. My favourite item is a short piano work—a musical snippet signed "Ed.E", and dated September 2, 1885, which he composed at Giggleswick for Mrs Buck. She and Elgar got on very well together, the young musician writing in 1888: "...I heard from Alice Beare that Mrs B is taking violently to the piano: I will bring something for her to play." The score he dedicated to her is important because little music for the piano was written by Elgar. Those who have heard it make comparisons with Schumann. Another version of this piece, *Griffinesque,* is dated February 17, 1884. I like the composition because it is cheerful and, I believe, reflects the atmosphere of the Buck household at Giggleswick when Young Mr Elgar came to stay for a few days.

Buck received tickets for concerts when Elgar was due to attend the Leeds Festival. In one accompanying letter, Elgar wrote puckishly: "Act decent and don't smoke during the Music." The letters which Elgar wrote to Buck—generally light and amusing, with lots of exclamation marks—have been preserved. The last letters were exchanged in 1932, when Buck was in what proved to be his terminal illness. Elgar survived until 1934.

Monica, as a small girl, had sat on Elgar's knee during a visit to the North. She treasured a chair which Elgar had given to her father, and which had a mechanism to allow one who used it to recline. He or she might also fix a movable music stand to either of the arms.

Among the musical fragments found following her death was a spoof piece of music sent by three cousins which surely evoked the Elgarian spirit of jest. The piece, said to have been written by Mouseorgski, was described as 'a parrot tune', recalling a time when Elgar and Buck had kidnapped Miss

Buck's parrot, had borne it down to Settle and, while crossing the bridge, had the embarrassment of seeing the bottom
of the cage fall out and a bemused parrot looking up at them
from the pavement. It was for many years a tale related by the
Buck family and their friends.

The music has a strong affinity with another Russian composer's *Big Gate at Kiev* from *Pictures at an Exhibition*.

Songs of the Settle-Carlisle

FOR seven long years, in the 1870s, North Ribblesdale and the topmost reaches of Wensleydale echoed to the sounds of railway-building. The Midland Company, determined to have a share of the lucrative Scottish traffic, using its own tracks, adapted a scheme put forward locally for a line to Hawes by obtaining Parliamentary approval for one between Settle and Carlisle, with a branch to Hawes, where it would join up with the North Eastern.

The work was labour-intensive. The contractors recruited labour from wherever it could be had. The number peaked at about six thousand for the entire enterprise. In the remotest parts, such as the bleak fell-country between Ribblehead and the head of Wensleydale, hutments which were to assume the grand name of 'shanty towns' were built to house and retain the men, who in many cases were joined by their families. A typical long wooden hut would have three rooms—one for the family, another for the lodgers and the central room for meals and general activity.

Mr Ashwell, who had obtained Contract No 1, also built a Mission Room at Ribblehead. It was served by Mr Tiplady, a missionary appointed by the Midland and Bradford City Mission. Sankey-type hymns were sung at the Sunday services. On Saturday evenings, Penny Readings were popular, the programme consisting of popular songs of the day, interspersed with verse, some evoking laughter and others stimulating tears.

Subsequently, religious services were held regularly in the waiting rooms at Ribblehead and Garsdale. At Ribblehead, the Vicar of Ingleton arrived at monthly intervals. Hymns were sung to the wheezy strains of a harmonium. Occasional dances were held in the waiting room, the music being provided by gramophone records brought by George Horner, of Salt Lake Cottages.

A *Daily Express* reporter, visiting the station at Garsdale Head in the summer of 1937, attended a monthy service of the type which was a feature of local life for fifty years. The officiating clergyman, Rev F G Baldrick, arrived carrying a little bag holding his miniature communion plate and vestments. The reporter found "the station platform was deserted, except for the sudden roar of a train on its way to Scotland...Then dim organ music came from the waiting-room. Women's voices sang a hymn."

Signalman George Gamsby had loaned the vicar a small harmonium. He and a porter carried it up to the platform and installed it at one end of the waiting room. Mrs Wilson, wife of a railway foreman, distributed the hymn books. She also laid a cloth over a small table which served as an altar. The bishop had given permission for communion to be celebrated. A lectern was the only other furniture in the oil-lit waiting-room. "They sang with vigour, standing in front of railway posters advertising holiday resorts. Their voices carried across the valley, the narrow River Clough running through it, to the fells beyond."

A room under the water tank at Garsdale station was a social centre for the railway families and for residents at the wide-flung farms and cottages of Garsdale parish. In the Tank House a wooden floor had been laid and efforts made to decorate the place. At concerts, in the 1930s, Mary Harper sang to a piano accompaniment provided by Mr D May, the stationmaster. Dances, concerts and whist drives provided winter enjoyment and raised money for charity.

Mike Donald

Mike Donald wrote his first song about the Settle-Carlisle railway in 1970. It took him just ten minutes to capture the spirit of the men who were constructing the line—whose job was to 'lay another rail'. David Joy and I played a very small part in the success of that song, for Mike had been inspired by reading our book about this famous fell-top railway. *The Dalesman* eventually issued the song, and others with a Dales flavour, as an LP record.

Mike told me he had gone to great pains to ensure that the words were historically accurate. "I just could not believe that trains were blown to a halt by gales at Ribblehead, so I talked with some old drivers and found that this was indeed so." As northern area manager for E J Arnold & Son., Ltd., the Leeds-based firm of education suppliers and publishers, Mike took up song-writing partly because he felt there was scope for songs to be used educationally. Schoolchildren most certainly responded to the lively strains of his musical record of the *Settle-Carlisle Railway.*

This song led to his first television appearance, on Border TV. Soon afterwards, in a second song, *Land of the Old and Grey,* he told of young people who were having to leave the Dales through economic necessity:

The Settle-Carlisle Railway

by Mike Donald

In the year of six - ty - nine they planned to run a train—— From Set- tle to Car - lisle—— a - cross the moun-tain range.———— They em-ployed three thou-sand nav - ies to build this might- y road———— And a-cross the fells thro' Ap -ple- by that old steam en-gine rolled. And it's up in the morn-ing,lads, in wind, snow,or hail. Hold fast to your ham-mers, lads, and lay an-oth-er rail.——————— 2. It's

I am a man of this land.
Thirty long years or more I have worked the Mallerstang Fells,
Never asked for more.
Young folks keep moving away:
Who can get them to stay?
There's money and there's jobs in the wool towns of the valleys.
This is the land of the old and grey.

Mike composed the song when returning from Appleby to Skipton by train at Christmas-time, 1969. He followed it with *The Swaledale Miners' Song* and *The Terrible Knitters of Dent*. Unlike the original ten-minute effort, he was now spending at least a month on each composition. His first record, a seven-inch LP, was released by the Yorkshire Dales Railway Society, a group who were hoping to establish a working transport museum at Embsay station, near Skipton. The main 'track' on this record was, of course, *Settle-Carlisle Railway*.

Subsequently, Mike was in great demand as a singer and entertainer. His talents were warmly applauded at *Yorkshire Neets* held in the Viking Hotel at York, where he met many visitors from overseas. He told me: "We have traditional Yorkshire food—Filey Coble Stew, Yorkshire Pudding, Roast Beef, Wensleydale Cheese and Old Peculiar Ales." Meanwhile Mike tapped a rich vein of Dales humour. My favourite among his stories was of a vicar's comment about the new organist: "We've had some bad organists in this church. Some couldn't read music. This latest chap is so bad he can't even read the words."

Mike's sudden death, when in the prime of life, was a great loss not only to his family and friends but also to Dales folk music.

Dave Goulder

A native of a village on the Notts/Derby border, Dave left school at the age of fifteen and eventually drifted into railways. He worked at various times as a porter, engine-cleaner, fireman, steam-raiser, tube-cleaner and knocker-up. The last position was so undemanding, he taught himself how to play the Spanish guitar while on the night shift. Simultaneously, he strung a few verses together. They were on railway topics.

When Dave Goulder climbed down from the footplate of a Class 8F for the last time in 1961, British Railways lost a mediocre fireman but the music world gained a highly individual writer and performer. From a new base in the Scottish Highlands, where he ran hostels for mountaineers and occasionally toured folk song clubs in the south, Dave viewed the passing age of steam with compassion and humour.

Dave then turned to his old hobby of drystone walling as a further means of earning a living. Soon he had his Master Craftsman certificate and had become instructor to the Agricultural Training Board for the Highlands and Islands, touring the area on a motor cycle to provide basic training in this ancient craft.

His first collection of railway songs was *Requiem for Steam* (1971). Critics were divided in their opinions, but all agreed on its originality of content. His song *The Settle and Carlisle,* which was published by the English Folk Dance and Song Society, who hold the copyright, is heart-rending.

Dave issued an LP of railway songs under the title *The Man Who Put the Engine in the Chip Shop,* one critic observing: "His clever rhymes and gentle melodies are engaging stuff..." Dave has also written and performed songs based on boyhood experiences of life in a rural area at a time when there were still a few horses to do the work.

I first met Dave at Skipton, then at Settle, as he took part in a revue, *Running Down the Line,* a celebration of the

The Settle & Carlisle

by Dave Goulder

The Settle Carlisle Rail..way was built in..to the Land; More
via...ducts and tun...nels than the Lines up...on your hand... She
cuts ac..ross the Pen..nines, ov..er wa..ter, rock and air.
Seven..ty miles of mon..u...ment to the men who put them
there.... I'd like to sit a.. while by the Settle and Car..lisle, And
delve a...mong the memories at eve...... ning...

"The Settle and Carlisle"

The Settle Carlisle Railway was built into the land
More viaducts and tunnels than the lines upon your hand
She cuts across the Pennines over water, rock and air
Seventy miles of monument to the men who put her there

> Chorus: *I'd like to sit awhile, by the Settle and Carlisle*
> *And delve among the memories at evening...*

You can feel the ghosts of engineers who first surveyed the line
Or conjure up a Jubilee or lumbering number nine
Or maybe find the water-troughs on a Garsdale afternoon
And listen to them filling when the Waverley has gone

Chorus

Cascades of falling water down the sides of Pen-y-ghent
And at the foot of Ingleborough,
    a solitary tent
The bridges over Arten Gill,
    Dent Head and Batty Moss
And silhouettes of steamers as they haul the trains across

Chorus

When snow is blown around the fells,
    the cuttings disappear
The tunnels fill with icicles,
    the line is never clear
But weather is a fickle thing,
    and snow will turn to rain
And the land slides all too easily;
    the digging starts again.

Chorus

When engine spotters gather here on summer Saturdays
Jostling with the travellers who go their different ways
The polished brass and uniforms of Settle's age of gold
But memories of better times are difficult to hold

Chorus

An engine on the turntable,
    the crew are climbing down
But dreams become reality as they start to turn her round
For the men turn into shadows,
    and the cinders into grass
And the engine's still revolving as it fades into the past

Chorus

famous railway, its history, landscape, character and humour, featuring Liz Humphrey-Williams, Mike Bettison and Ritchie Taylor. It was something quite new. Mike sat on a plinth and contributed the songs, one of them having the title *Ais Gill,* which as every Settle-Carlisle enthusiast knows, is the place where the line reaches its highest point.

Jan Holdstock

When the staff and scholars of Catteral Hall, the preparatory school for Giggleswick, were celebrating their sixtieth anniversary, and were hosts for the Northern Preparatory Schools' Music Day, in 1994, a cantata was commissioned from Jan Holdstock, of Leeds. Entitled *Running on Rails,* it dealt with the building of the Settle-Carlisle Railway. I had the honour of giving a narration which had been written by Pat Belford.

The world premiere of *Running on Rails* was given by a choir of 120, representing Aysgarth, Malsis Hall, Ripon Cathedral Choir School and Catteral Hall. Simon Lindley, organist and choirmaster at Leeds Parish Church, conducted the first performance.

With piano and drums providing an accompaniment, and Simon urging the young choristers to ever-greater efforts, the songs lived. *Seventy Two Miles of Rail* ended with an appropriate *shhhh* (as the locomotive came to a halt at Carlisle). *Pennine Weather Song* (see page 6) provided a contrast between languid summer days and a winter when the snow 'freezes and it flurries'.

As narrator, my greatest moment came in the run-up to a calypso referring to ''a wonderful new invention, costing £200 per ton'' which ''was transported by road to the hills for blasting the rock...its name was Dynamite!'' A second later, Simon and the young choristers began *Dynamite Calypso* with an appropriate explosion of sound.

Then:

> Light the fuse and then beware.
> It's dynamite, so you must take care.

During the singing, I glanced to where the composer was sitting. Her feet were tapping. The choir itself was following Simon Lindley's injunction to look happy. A cantata called *Running on Rails* had (musically) stayed on the track.

Stan Chandler

Stanley Edward Chandler is a Glaswegian who was educated in Nottingham and took a BSc degree at Sheffield University. He spent his working life, up to taking early retirement in 1996, in the public sector. Stan has written about 250 hymns, setting his own tunes to the majority of them.

His enthusiasm for the Settle-Carlisle dates from just before Christmas in 1983 when he read of a proposal to close the famous railway. The Friends of the Settle-Carlisle line had been formed in 1981 to galvanise support for the retention of the line. For Stan there was the terrible prospect of never again being able to travel over this railway which links two north-south valleys with a spectacular High Fell section.

Stan writes: "My own use of the line is purely for recreation, but I was aware how vital was the line to the folk living in the scattered towns and villages which it served." He registered an objection to the closure and was impelled to compose a collection of hymns and tunes, which were published in March, 1990. "I had a deep personal conviction that the line would be spared and thankfully this has been the case."

I have selected the hymn entitled *Ribblehead*.

Ribblehead

by Stan Chandler

7 7.7 7.7 7. (23-5-86)

Moorland Interludes

ARTHUR Butterworth has developed many of his musical themes while walking on the moors—solitary but never lonely. A Mancunian, he began his formal musical studies at the Royal Manchester College of Music, following military service, and he became a professional orchestral trumpeter in the Scottish National Orchestra. He then returned to Manchester to join the Halle Orchestra.

Success as a composer was first attained forty years ago, in 1957, when Sir John Barbirolli conducted the premiere of the young composer's First Symphony. This work brought wide recognition which enabled him to relinquish the demanding life of an orchestral player and devote far more time to composition, though he became active as an orchestral conductor. Composition is the occupation for which he is best known.

His work most closely relates in style and intention to that of Sibelius (1865-1957), though apart from this essentially nordic influence he has followed in the wake of English composers of the earlier part of this century. As a conductor, he has a particular predilection for Elgar, directing many performances of the music of this greatest of all English composers.

Living in the Dales, Arthur Butterworth has a keen interest in wildlife, painting, in oils and also water-colours, and industrial archaeology, not least a contemplation of the glories of the Settle-Carlisle railway. An early work, *The Path to the Moors*, for orchestra, was written in Manchester and came out of many walks over the moors between Huddersfield, Halifax and Oldham—the rather bleak and sometimes forbidding grey moorland landscape which is so characteristic of the Brontes. In contrast is *The Quiet Tarn*, an orchestral piece first played by the BBC Northern Orchestra (now the BBC

Philharmonic) and inspired by what he refers to as "the glorious 1st June, 1959, and a first visit to Malham Tarn." It was for Arthur the virtual beginning of his love affair with the Yorkshire Dales.

A Dales Suite, written from home at Embsay, within easy view of Embsay Crag and the shaggy moors at the edge of the Bolton Abbey estate, was written in 1964 for the band of Ermysted's Grammar School, Skipton, and later transcribed for the BBC Concert Orchestra. *The Moors,* his suite for a large orchestra and organ, was first played by the BBC Northern Orchestra in 1962. For *A Moorland Symphony,* he returned in spirit to the South Pennines and the verse of Ammon Wrigley (1870-1946), the Saddleworth poet, being first performed by the local Music Society and a section of the BBC Northern Orchestra at Uppermill, 1967.

The Night Wind, a song-cycle commissioned by the Arts Council of Great Britain for the Calder Valley Festival of 1969, was inspired by the poems of Emily Bronte and features soprano, clarinet and piano. It was later transcribed for orchestra and performed at the Queen Elizabeth Hall by the Bournemouth Sinfonietta, 1970. This was followed by *September Morn,* a work for a large orchestra, the music being commissioned by the Arts Council in 1983 but so far unperformed. *Winter Music,* for brass band, was commissioned by the Queensbury Band (not the Black Dyke Mills) in 1980 and was later transcribed for a large wind band. *Summer Music* is a bassoon concerto, which was first performed by the Settle Orchestra, of which Arthur was the conductor for many years, at Giggleswick Church in 1987. *The Viola Concerto,* first performed by the BBC Philharmonic in 1993, harked back in its conception to a night under the stars by Malham Tarn in 1988.

Northern Light, commissioned by the Leeds Symphony Orchestra for its centenary in 1992, is an impression of a summer dawn on the high moors and *The Symphony No 4* arose from a contemplation of the northern moorlands in

1 – PRELUDE

"A Dales Suite"

Arthur Butterworth Op. 24b.

November, this piece being first played by the BBC Philharmonic in 1986. Most recently is the composer's *String Quartet* (Opus 100), which recalls in purely abstract musical terms— that is, with no specific 'programme'—the essence of midsummer nights on the high moorlands. So recent is this quartet, which was completed in July 1997, it has not been rehearsed or performed.

Arthur Butterworth's regard for the music of Elgar, and his long association with the Settle Orchestra, has enabled him to compare the type of orchestra conducted by C W Buck, who was several times host to Elgar at Giggleswick, with the Orchestra of today. Buck conducted the local operatic society orchestra, made up of people living within easy distance of the Victoria Hall, a core of instrumentalists being among his special friends who gathered regularly in his music room, at the back of the house, to play instruments in an atmosphere thick with pipe-smoke.

Buck's orchestra was probably moulded on the lines of a pier orchestra. The music was light and unpretentious, with popular selections of all kinds and hardly anything which was intellectual or syphonic. Precise instrumentation did not really matter. Things were watered-down from the composers' original scorings. There would be just enough string players to provide one or two players for each part, instead of the now familiar ten or more First Violins, eight or ten Seconds, six or more Violas and 'Cellos, and two or three Double basses. Most local amateur orchestras were of similar modest proportions.

When Arthur Butterworth took over Settle Orchestra in 1969, it was very much a re-birth of Buck's orchestra of all those years before, though by this time, with much improved transport, the society was able to draw on musicians from various parts of the far-flung district of Craven. Within a few years, its direction had changed. The players, though essentially amateur, had heard radio and recorded performances of great orchestras and aspired to do the same kind of challenging repertoire. "We counted it as something of a landmark when in the late 1970s it was possible to perform Elgar's *Enigma Variations*—a masterpiece suited to a large modern orchestra, including an organ, the venue being Skipton Parish Church."

The present day Settle Orchestra can call upon all the necessary extra instruments. Gone are the days when, for example, percussionists were drably referred to as 'drums and effects'. The problem today is still in finding enough really good string players. In this, Settle is like almost all other amateur orchestras, for whereas wind-playing has improved by leaps and bounds over the past thirty or more years, string-playing is still the most difficult of instrumental arts.

In March, 1997, the Settle Orchestra, under the baton of Howard Rogerson, and with Anne Heaton as leader, presented a concert of English music at Ingleton.

In Recent Years

THE hills and dales are alive with the sound of music. The initiatives of the West Riding County Council when introducing visiting instrumental tuition into schools have joyously increased and at the moment over 7,000 young people aged from eight to eighteen years, are developing skills by playing in an orchestra or a band or some solo instrument such as a guitar. Far from causing a decline in numbers, the introduction of a small fee towards the costs of lessons led to an expansion of the service, with a greater number of teachers reaching pupils in more schools.

In North Yorkshire, the main music centres are based in Harrogate and Northallerton, where pupils from these towns, and many from the dale-country, make music in a range of ensembles which match their interests and abilities. Some 400 talented young musicians make music on Saturday mornings at each Centre and occasionally perform in prestigious venues such as the Harrogate International Conference Centre. Skipton Music Centre has about 150 young musicians who regularly play in ensembles. As they make progress, they may join either the Harrogate and Skipton Symphony Orchestra or the Harrogate and Skipton Area Band. A recent innovative feature is the Harrogate Young Jazz orchestra.

The annual Music Day at Fountains Abbey and Studley Royal illustrates, as much as any single event, the diversity of music with local associations. The Abbey, West Green and Fountains Hall resound to music through the ages, performed by choirs, bands, solo instrumentalists and teams of folk and morris dancers. Visitors hear the sounds of harps and shawms, saxophones, fiddles and accordions. They listen to sacred and secular music, from medieval motets and

Jacobean madigrals, Baroque and Victorian melodies, to modern compositions. Two lively morris sides in colourful costumes and with painted faces celebrate in dance a tradition dating back to pre-Christian times.

The annual Grassington Festival, in Wharfedale, has brought world-class musicians to perform in the very heart of the Dales. Concertgoers have listened appreciatively to Russians, Americans, Chinese and others from the Orient, as well as British artistes of the front rank. The Festival has featured serious music and popular musical entertainment alike. It is all part of an upsurge of musical talent and skill which is a fairly recent feature of the rural musical scene. Music features in the Swaledale Festival, which is held bi-annually, and periodically high quality musical events are held in Askrigg Church, Wensleydale. Ilkley has a range of musical activity, including a splendid Wind Band.

Valerie Boulard conducts the highly successful Langcliffe Singers, in North Ribblesdale. A solitary fiddler, so important in old-time Dales music-making, was recruited to record music for a play written by Barbara Slater and performed at Threshfield School in Wharfedale, the plot concerning the resident ghost, Old Pam, whose fiddle-playing is said to have driven the local Rector so mad he killed him. Pam (and the fiddle) returned to haunt the place. Tim Boothman, a keen violinist and student of old-time Dales music, recorded the fiddle-music. Artesan, of Huddersfield, have set much of the Dales verse of Dorothy Una Ratcliffe into music.

Many distinguished former professional musicians who live in the Dales include William and Valerie Leary, both former members of the London Philharmonic Orchestra, who for some years lived at Gargrave and have recently moved to Ampleforth College, stimulating string music of world-class standard, with the support of organist Simon Wright. In Harrogate lives William Lang, trumpeter of distinction and one-time principal cornet of the Black Dyke Mills Band, being in recent years the principal trumpet of the London Symphony

Orchestra. Mr Lang was in his youth a master stone-craftsman. Now, in retirement from music, he again practises the art of working with stone. From Littleport, near Ripon, comes the harpist Georgina Wells, now making a career in London and the United States.

Skipton Music Society, now over fifty years old, programmes celebrated artists from Europe and America—pianists, string quartets, solo singers, chamber ensembles, organists, wind groups, baroque music groups and, in one recent season, a brass band. These Tuesday concerts attract a capacity audience to Skipton Town Hall, as do the events promoted by the Ilkley Concerts Club on Wednesdays.

The high mobility made possible through improved roads and the transport revolution has enabled players and singers to converge on Dales venues from a wide area. The hills and dales are, indeed, alive with the sound of music.

Acknowledgements

Many people have co-operated in the production of this book. Special thanks are extended to Chris Alderson, J L Barker, Margaret Batty, BBC (The Archers), Agnes Beswick, Helen Brassington, Duncan Bythell, Jim Calvert, Stan Chandler, D J Cherry, Alice Cowking, Dalesman Publishing Company, Darlington and Stockton Times, Roma Dinsdale, Pauline Donald, Alice Fawcett, Dave Goulder, Doris Hartley, Marie Hartley MBE, Harrogate Library, Joan Ingilby MBE, Ralph Lake, Valerie Langfield, Elizabeth Middleton, David Morris, David Parkinson, Senior Adviser, Music, North Yorkshire County Council, Irene Porter, Mike Porter, Enid Pyrah, Laurie Rukin, Jennifer and George Wallis, Doris Wells.

Line Illustrations

Pateley Bridge Cockoo, Ernest Forbes, 1. Title Page Illustration, © Reginald Napier, 3. A Daleswoman (Fred Lawson, Author's collection), 87. Dent (Peter Fox), 114. Impression of Delius, based on photograph and used for a Delius Festival in Bradford, 129. Edward Elgar, based on a photograph (Author's collection), 139. Mouse-orgski's parrot-tune, sent to Monica Buck (Author's collection), 142. Settle-Carlisle drawing (Peter Fox), 143.

Music

Pennine Weather Song, by Jan Holdstock, © Catteral Hall, Giggleswick, courtesy of the headmaster, Martin J Morris, 6. Extract from The White Cockade, as recorded at West Witton and published in The Music of the Yorkshire Dales (1931) by J Sutcliffe Smith, 20. Christmas in the Dale. Words and music by Mike Donald. © Mike Donald, 1976, courtesy of Pauline Donald, 24. Beautiful Swaledale, the Land of Rest, traditional Swaledale song, score as noted by Jennifer Wallis, 30. Beautiful Dale, Home of the Swale, traditional song, score as noted by Jennifer Wallis, 32. Lily Dale, traditional song as noted by Jennifer Wallis, 37. Sweet Lass of Richmond Hill, from the old song written by Leonard MacNally (1789) and set to music by James Hook, 43. Gunnerside, hymn tune composed by Jas Reynoldson, kindly loaned by his daughter, Mrs Matthew Cherry, 60. Harmonisation by

Edward Elgar of ballad about Yorkshire horse-dealers collected by Charles William Buck. Donated by Author with original Giggleswick scores of Elgar to Elgar Foundation, 69-70. Kendal Ghyll, folk tune collected in the Dales by Leta Douglas and published in Six Dances of the Yorkshire Dales (1931), 76. Huntsman's Chorus, ditto, 80. Muker, hymn tune composed by Jas Reynoldson (reproduced courtesy of his daughter, Mrs Cherry), 93. Ilkla' Moor, song using the old hymn tune Cranbrook for its musical setting, 99. Tarry Woo', traditional north-country song used by Betty Hartley and Elizabeth Middleton when demonstrating Dent-style knitting, 105. Knit, knit, knit, traditional song, used at Mary Wakefield Festival over sixty years ago, 113. Ballad of Swaledale, Ken Briggs, 114. Wigglesworth, hymn tune written by Alice Fawcett (and reproduced with her kind permission), 121. St Alkelda, composed by R Barrett Watson (1904) for the organ of Giggleswick Church, 124. Letter from Roger Quilter to Jack Brassington, courtesy of family, 137. The Settle-Carlisle Railway, by Mike Donald, courtesy of Pauline Donald, © EFDSS, 146. The Settle & Carlisle, by Dave Goulder, courtesy of Dave Goulder, © EFDSS Music, 149 (music), 150 (words). Ribblehead, by Stan Chandler, © Stan Chandler, 3 Aldam Croft, Totley, Sheffield, S17 4GF, 153. A Dales Suite, Arthur Butterworth © Arthur Butterworth, 1981), 157. Vesper, by H Lord, 154.

Every effort has been made to ensure copyright clearance. The author would be pleased to be informed of any accidental infringement so the matter can be addressed.

Photographs

Front cover—Bugle being blown at Settle at a gathering to compete for the Ancient Scorton Arrow (Author). Back cover—Settle Orchestra in Settle Market Place following the unveiling of a plaque to Edward Elgar (Enid Pyrah).

Raking hay near Thwaite (Author), 57. Thomas Joy on Grassington Moor (from a photograph in Joy's collection copied by the Author), 58. Swaledale sheep, Hubberholme Church (Author), 58. Cecil Slingsby, 59. Leta Douglas (photograph loaned by Miss Onyx Ralph), 59. Handel Parker, composer of Deep Harmony (loaned by Dr Ian Dewhirst), 59. Harry Cockerill (Author), 60.